AAT

Advanced Bookkeeping

Level 3

Advanced Diploma in

Accounting

Question Bank

Fourth edition 2018

ISBN 9781 5097 1873 3

British Library Cataloguing-in-Publication Data
A catalogue record for this book is available
from the British Library

Published by

BPP Learning Media Ltd
BPP House, Aldine Place
142-144 Uxbridge Road
London W12 8AA

www.bpp.com/learningmedia

Printed in the United Kingdom

Your learning materials, published by BPP Learning
Media Ltd, are printed on paper obtained from
traceable sustainable sources.

A note about copyright

Contents

Introduction

This is BPP Learning Media's AAT Question Bank for *Advanced Bookkeeping*. It is part of a suite of ground-breaking resources produced by BPP Learning Media for AAT assessments.

This Question Bank has been written in conjunction with the BPP Course Book, and has been carefully designed to enable students to practise all of the learning outcomes and assessment criteria for *Advanced Bookkeeping*. It is fully up to date as at June 2017 and reflects both the AAT's qualification specification and the sample assessment provided by the AAT.

This Question Bank contains these key features:

- Tasks corresponding to each chapter of the Course Book. Some tasks are designed for learning purposes, others are of assessment standard

- AAT's AQ2016 sample assessments 1 and 2 for *Advanced Bookkeeping* with answers and further BPP practice assessments

The emphasis in all tasks and assessments is on the practical application of the skills acquired.

VAT

You may find tasks throughout this Question Bank that need you to calculate or be aware of a rate of VAT. This is stated at 20% in these examples and questions.

Approaching the assessment

When you sit the assessment it is very important that you follow the on screen instructions. This means you need to carefully read the instructions, both on the introduction screens and during specific tasks.

When you access the assessment you should be presented with an introductory screen with information similar to that shown below (taken from the introductory screen from the AAT's AQ2016 sample assessments for *Advanced Bookkeeping*).

We have provided this **sample assessment** to help you familiarise yourself with our e-assessment environment. It is designed to demonstrate as many as possible of the question types that you may find in a live assessment. It is not designed to be used on its own to determine whether you are ready for a live assessment.

Assessment information:

You have **2 hours** to complete this sample assessment.

This assessment contains **5 tasks** and you should attempt to complete **every** task.
Each task is independent. You will not need to refer to your answers to previous tasks.
Read every task carefully to make sure you understand what is required.

The standard rate of VAT is 20%.

Where the date is relevant, it is given in the task data.
Both minus signs and brackets can be used to indicate negative numbers **unless** task instructions say otherwise.

You must use a full stop to indicate a decimal point. For example, write 100.57 NOT 100,57 or 100 57
You may use a comma to indicate a number in the thousands, but you don't have to. For example 10000 and 10,000 are both acceptable.

The actual instructions will vary depending on the subject you are studying for. It is very important you read the instructions on the introductory screen and apply them in the assessment. You don't want to lose marks when you know the correct answer just because you have not entered it in the right format.

In general, the rules set out in the AAT sample assessments for the subject you are studying for will apply in the real assessment, but you should carefully read the information on this screen again in the real assessment, just to make sure. This screen may also confirm the VAT rate used if applicable.

A full stop is needed to indicate a decimal point. We would recommend using minus signs to indicate negative numbers and leaving out the comma signs to indicate thousands, as this results in a lower number of key strokes and less margin for error when working under time pressure. Having said that, you can use whatever is easiest for you as long as you operate within the rules set out for your particular assessment.

You have to show competence throughout the assessment and you should therefore complete all of the tasks. Don't leave questions unanswered.

In some assessments, written or complex tasks may be human marked. In this case you are given a blank space or table to enter your answer into. You are told in the assessments which tasks these are (note: may be none if all answers are marked by the computer).

If these involve calculations, it is a good idea to decide in advance how you are going to lay out your answers to such tasks by practising answering them on a word document, and certainly you should try all such tasks in this Question Bank and in the AAT's environment using the sample assessment.

When asked to fill in tables, or gaps, never leave any blank even if you are unsure of the answer. Fill in your best estimate.

Note that for some assessments where there is a lot of scenario information or tables of data provided (eg tax tables), you may need to access these via 'pop-ups'. Instructions will be provided on how you can bring up the necessary data during the assessment.

Finally, take note of any task specific instructions once you are in the assessment. For example you may be asked to enter a date in a certain format or to enter a number to a certain number of decimal places.

Grading

To achieve the qualification and to be awarded a grade, you must pass all the mandatory unit assessments, all optional unit assessments (where applicable) and the synoptic assessment.

The AAT Level 3 Advanced Diploma in Accounting will be awarded a grade. This grade will be based on performance across the qualification. Unit assessments and synoptic assessments are not individually graded. These assessments are given a mark that is used in calculating the overall grade.

How overall grade is determined

You will be awarded an overall qualification grade (Distinction, Merit, and Pass). If you do not achieve the qualification you will not receive a qualification certificate, and the grade will be shown as unclassified.

The marks of each assessment will be converted into a percentage mark and rounded up or down to the nearest whole number. This percentage mark is then weighted according to the weighting of the unit assessment or synoptic assessment within the qualification. The resulting weighted assessment percentages are combined to arrive at a percentage mark for the whole qualification.

Grade definition	Percentage threshold
Distinction	90–100%
Merit	80–89%
Pass	70–79%
Unclassified	0–69% Or failure to pass one or more assessment/s

Re-sits

Some AAT qualifications such as the AAT Advanced Diploma in Accounting have restrictions in place for how many times you are able to re-sit assessments. Please refer to the AAT website for further details.

You should only be entered for an assessment when you are well prepared and you expect to pass the assessment.

AAT qualifications

The material in this book may support the following AAT qualifications:

AAT Advanced Diploma in Accounting Level 3, AAT Advanced Diploma in Accounting at SCQF Level 6 and Further Education and Training Certificate: Accounting Technician (Level 4 AATSA).

Supplements

From time to time we may need to publish supplementary materials to one of our titles. This can be for a variety of reasons, including minor changes to the AAT unit guidance or new legislation coming into effect between editions.

You should check our supplements page regularly for anything that may affect your learning materials. All supplements are available free of charge on our supplements page on our website at:

www.bpp.com/learning-media/about/students

Improving material and removing errors

There is a constant need to update and enhance our study materials in line with both regulatory changes and new insights into the assessments.

From our team of authors BPP appoints a subject expert to update and improve these materials for each new edition.

Their updated draft is subsequently technically checked by another author and from time to time non-technically checked by a proof reader.

We are very keen to remove as many numerical errors and narrative typos as we can but given the volume of detailed information being changed in a short space of time we know that a few errors will sometimes get through our net.

We apologise in advance for any inconvenience that an error might cause. We continue to look for new ways to improve these study materials and would welcome your suggestions. If you have any comments about this book, please email nisarahmed@bpp.com or write to Nisar Ahmed, AAT Head of Programme, BPP Learning Media Ltd, BPP House, Aldine Place, London W12 8AA.

Question Bank

Chapter 1 – Bookkeeping transactions

Task 1.1

Compete the sentences below by selecting the appropriate option from the picklist.

The sales returns day book lists	▼
The purchases day book lists	▼
The purchases returns day book lists	▼
The sales day book lists	▼

Picklist:

invoices sent to customers
credit notes sent to customers
invoices received from suppliers
credit notes received from suppliers

Task 1.2

Record the double entry for each of the following transactions of a business:

(a) **Payment of £15,000 into a business bank account by the owner in order to start up the business.**

Account		Debit £	Credit £
	▼		
	▼		

(b) **Payment by cheque of £2,000 for the rent of a business property.**

Account		Debit £	Credit £
	▼		
	▼		

(c) **Payment by cheque of £6,200 for the purchase of goods for resale.**

Account		Debit £	Credit £
	▼		
	▼		

(d) **Payment by cheque of £150 for electricity.**

Account		Debit £	Credit £
	▼		
	▼		

Picklist:

Balance b/d
Balance c/d
Bank
Capital
Electricity
Purchases
Purchases ledger control account
Rent

Task 1.3

A new business has the following transactions:

(1) Receipt of £20,000 capital into the bank account from the owner
(2) Payment by cheque of £2,100 for goods for resale
(3) Sold goods for £870 cash
(4) Purchase of goods for resale on credit for £2,800
(5) Sale of goods on credit for £3,400
(6) Payment by cheque of £1,500 to credit suppliers
(7) Receipt of cheque from credit customer of £1,600

Enter the transactions into the accounts below. Balance off the accounts. As appropriate, show clearly the:

- **Balance to be carried down and brought down; or**
- **Balance to be transferred to the profit or loss account.**

Bank

	£		£
		▼	
▼		▼	
▼		▼	
▼		▼	

Capital

	£		£
▼		▼	
▼		▼	

Purchases

	£		£
▼		▼	
▼		▼	

Purchases ledger control account

	£		£
▼		▼	
▼		▼	
▼		▼	

Sales

	£		£
▼		▼	
▼		▼	

Sales ledger control account

	£			£
	▼		▼	
	▼		▼	
	▼		▼	

Picklist:

Balance b/d
Balance c/d
Bank
Capital
Profit or loss account
Purchases
Purchases ledger control account
Sales
Sales ledger control account

Task 1.4

Complete the initial trial balance by entering the balances in the debit or credit columns, as appropriate. Total the trial balance.

Trial balance	Amount £	Debit £	Credit £
Bank (positive balance)	11,000		
Capital	14,000		
Electricity	2,000		
Purchases	4,500		
Purchases ledger control account	3,000		
Rent (expense)	2,500		
Sales	9,000		
Sales ledger control account	12,000		
VAT control account (due to HMRC)	6,000		

BPP
LEARNING MEDIA

Task 1.5

The following items are included in the VAT control account.

(a)   Show whether the balances will be debit or credit items on the VAT control account.

Ledger account	Amount £	Debit ✓	Credit ✓
Sales	13,000		
Sales returns	1,000		
Purchases	8,000		
Purchases returns	2,000		
Bank	3,500		

(b)   Calculate the amount owed to or due from HMRC at the end of the period. From the perspective of the business, indicate whether it is an asset or liability.

Amount owed at the end of the period: £	
Asset or liability	▼

Picklist:

Asset
Liability

Chapter 2 – Accounting principles

Task 2.1

There are two main types of non-current assets, intangible assets and tangible assets.

For each description, select the most appropriate term from the list below.

Description	Term
Assets which do not have a physical substance, for example licences and brands	▼
Assets which have a physical substance, for example property, plant and equipment	▼

Picklist:

Intangible assets
Tangible assets

Task 2.2

For each description, select the most appropriate term from the list below.

Description	Term
This shows what the business owes back to its owner.	▼
These relate to liabilities owed by the business due to its day-to-day activities and include trade payables, accruals, VAT owed to the tax authorities and bank overdrafts.	▼
These are costs that a business has incurred over the accounting period.	▼
These relate to assets used by the business on a day-to-day basis and include inventory, trade receivables and bank balances.	▼
Tangible or intangible assets held and used in the business over the long term (ie more than one year).	▼
These are amounts that the business has earned over the accounting period.	▼
These relate to the long-term debts of the business and include items such as long-term bank loans.	▼

Picklist:

Capital
Current assets
Current liabilities
Expenses
Income
Non-current assets
Non-current liabilities

. . . .

Task 2.3

Classify the following items as an asset, liability, income, expense or capital.

Item	Asset, liability, income, expense or capital
A laptop used in the accounts department of a retail store	▼
Equity interest	▼
A bank loan	▼

Picklist:

Asset
Capital
Expense
Income
Liability

. . . .

Task 2.4

Complete the sentence below by selecting the most appropriate option.

A credit balance on a general ledger account indicates

	✓
an asset, capital or an expense	
a liability or an expense	
an amount owing to the organisation	
a liability, capital or income	

Task 2.5

The scenarios take place within an accounting practice.

Identify the fundamental principle which is relevant to the scenarios below.

Both scenarios should be considered separately.

Scenarios	Fundamental principle
Employees who may receive a bonus depending on the financial performance of the accounting practice do not prepare the accounting practice's financial statements.	▼
The new trainee accounting technician is supervised by her manager and receives the necessary training.	▼

Picklist:

Confidentiality
Integrity
Objectivity
Professional behaviour
Professional competence and due care

Task 2.6

Wilson and Sons is a manufacturing business which holds a significant quantity of high value inventory.

Which organisational procedure will be used to safeguard the inventory?

Control procedures	✓
Physical controls	
Segregation of duties	
Authorisation of transactions	
Written record of procedures	

Task 2.7

Why does a business need to establish and follow organisational policies and procedures in relation to its accounting function?

Select ONE option.

	✓
To ensure that the accounting policies selected maximise the business's profits	
To ensure the accounting records truly reflect the transactions and financial results of the business	
To ensure that the business acts in the owner's best interests	
To minimise the tax payable on the business's profits	

Task 2.8

Campbell is a retailer with a number of high street stores. The business's owner suspects the checkout operator in one particular store of possible theft as the cash takings in that store are much lower than in all of the others.

Which type of organisational policy would be the most appropriate to put in place to detect missing cash in the store?

Select ONE option.

	✓
Review of budgeted to actual information	
Written record of procedures	
Physical controls	
Authorisation of transactions	

Task 2.9

Hill sells cutting edge technological products such as the latest tablets, laptops and smartphones. Inventory is stored in a central warehouse before being distributed to retail outlets or direct to customers who have ordered online.

Hill maintains computerised accounting records. You are the accounts supervisor. The junior bookkeeper has asked you why the accounting records are password protected and only the members of the accounts department and the business's owner have access to that password.

Which of the following can you use in your explanation to him?
Select ONE option for each row.

	Acceptable reason ✓	Not acceptable reason ✓
The business has high value desirable inventory, making the risk of theft high, which could be covered up by unauthorised alteration of accounting records.		
Only the accounts department are likely to have the necessary skills and knowledge to maintain the accounting records.		
The password will prevent anyone in the accounts department deliberately manipulating accounting records.		
The password will prevent theft of inventory and cash from the business.		

Task 2.10

You are working on the accounting records of a client for the year ended 30 June 20X6. The proprietor of the business has proposed that the following four adjustments be made before the accounts are finalised.

Which of the following adjustments appears genuine and should be included in the final accounts for the year ended 30 June 20X6?

Select ONE option.

	✓
A write down of a line of inventory at the year end from cost to NRV is it was sold at a loss in July 20X6	
A decrease in the allowance for doubtful debts because of a rise in the average number of days credit customers are taking to pay	
An increase in the useful life of plant and machinery to reduce the depreciation charge	
Posting a cash payment to the suspense account	

BPP
LEARNING MEDIA

Task 2.11

You are a trainee accounting technician reporting to a managing partner in an accounting practice. You are working on the accounting records of a client.

In which circumstance would it be appropriate to disclose information about your client without breaching the fundamental principle of confidentiality from the AAT's *Code of Professional Ethics*?

Select ONE option for each row.

	Appropriate ✓	Not appropriate ✓
Allowing the manager partner to review the year end accounts that you have prepared		
Emailing the accounts to your friend who is thinking of applying for a job with the client		
Allowing the client's bank to access the accounts with the proprietor's permission		
Allowing a credit supplier of your client access to the accounts when deciding whether or not to increase credit terms without authorisation from the proprietor		

Task 2.12

You work in an accounting practice and are preparing the year end accounts for a client. The client owns a very small business and prepares his own accounting records as he has completed Levels 1, 2 and 3 of his AAT studies.

When you are preparing the year end accounts, you notice that the proprietor of the business has taken £5,000 out of the business for his own personal use and has recorded the amount as an expense.

Which of the following statements are valid in respect of the above transaction?

Select ONE option for each row.

	Valid ✓	Not valid ✓
The accounting treatment is correct so there has been no breach of the AAT's *Code of Professional Ethics*.		
If this treatment was deliberate, there has been a breach of the fundamental principle of integrity.		
If this treatment was a genuine error, there has been a breach of the fundamental principle of professional competence and due care.		
There is a clear breach of confidentiality here requiring your firm to resign as accountants for this client.		

Task 2.13

You are a trainee accounting technician reporting to the managing partner in an accounting practice. You are working on the accounts of a business. The client is a longstanding friend of the managing partner and is godfather to the managing partner's youngest child.

Which of the threats to the AAT's *Code of Professional Ethics* is most relevant here?

Select ONE option.

	✓
Self-interest	
Self-review	
Advocacy	
Familiarity	
Intimidation	

Task 2.14

The following is a list of the business's assets and liabilities at the year end.

	£
Property, plant and equipment	120,000
Inventories	43,000
Trade receivables	65,000
Bank (positive balance)	16,400
Trade payables	57,100
Bank loan	32,000

What is the business's capital at the year end?

£

Task 2.15

At 1 January 20X6, a business had capital of £250,000. During the year ended 31 December 20X6, the following occurred:

- The business made a profit of £37,500
- The owner withdrew cash of £4,700 for his own personal use
- The owner injected new capital of £12,000 into the business

What was the amount of the business's net assets at 31 December 20X6?

£

Task 2.16

Which ONE of the following statements about the accounting equation is true?

	✓
Capital – Liabilities = Assets	
Double entry bookkeeping is based on the accounting equation	
All elements of the accounting equation can be found in the statement of profit or loss	
Closing capital = Opening capital – Profit + Drawings	

Task 2.17

A business makes a sale of £672 on credit to a long standing customer.

How will the elements of the accounting equation be affected by recording this transaction?

	Increase ✓	Decrease ✓	No change ✓
Assets			
Liabilities			
Capital			

Task 2.18

As an accounting technician, what is the most important reason for following organisational policies and procedures?

Choose ONE:

	✓
To ensure that you understand your responsibilities	
To ensure that the company meets all of its legal responsibilities	
To make it easy for you to complete your day-to-day tasks	
To improve your technical knowledge	

Task 2.19

Which ONE of these would be acceptable professional behaviour if actioned by you?

	✓
You have been asked to account for a provision but you are unsure how to do this, so you make a guess at the appropriate treatment.	
A client has given you tickets to a high profile football match. The next day they ask you to ignore the liquidation of a customer that owes the client a substantial amount of money.	
Your firm needs to meet its deadline in preparing the accounts. Your supervisor tells you to save time by just repeating the depreciation entry from last year, rather than recalculating it.	
The bank statement for your firm shows that an insurance bill covering the next accounting period has been paid in the current accounting period. Your manager asks you to make a prepayment for the cost of the insurance.	

Chapter 3 – Purchase of non-current assets

Task 3.1

A business has a policy of capitalising expenditure over £300. Ignore VAT.

In each of the following circumstances, determine how much capital expenditure has been incurred and how much revenue expenditure has been incurred by the business.

Expenditure	Capital expenditure £	Revenue expenditure £
A machine has been purchased at a cost of £12,000. The delivery charge was £400.		
A building has been purchased at a cost of £120,000. The building is subsequently redecorated at a cost of £13,000.		
A new main server has been purchased at a cost of £10,000. Professional fees of £200 were also incurred, as a result of this expenditure.		

Task 3.2

A business has a policy of capitalising expenditure over £500. The business is not registered for VAT.

The business acquires computer equipment for £48,000 (including VAT at 20%).

At what amount should the computer equipment be capitalised?

£	

Task 3.3

Match the descriptions to the relevant funding method by selecting from the picklist.

Description	Method
The vending machines in a business's premises were financed by paying an initial deposit to the finance company followed by a fixed number of instalments. After all instalments have been paid, the vending machines will be owned by the business.	▼
When a business purchases a new motor vehicle, the old vehicle is given to the dealer to cover part of the cost of the new vehicle.	▼
Factory equipment is acquired as part of a major refurbishment. The bank provides the funding, which is then paid back in instalments over an agreed period of time, together with interest.	▼

Picklist:

Cash purchase
Finance lease
Hire purchase
Loan
Part-exchange

Task 3.4

A business has a policy of capitalising expenditure over £500. You may ignore VAT in this task.

The following is an extract from a purchase invoice received by LBC Trading relating to new equipment for its head office.

To: LBC Trading 14 High Street, Hill Gate, HI2 4DN	Invoice 3728 Hugo & Sons 68 Arne Grove South Mines SM3 9MF	Date: 01 June 20X4
Item	**Details**	**£**
Boardroom table	HF405	10,500.00
Boardroom table fittings	HF405	2,600.00
Delivery costs	HF405	450.00
Boardroom chairs (5 items)	PN2948	300.00
Net total		13,850.00

The acquisition has been made under a finance lease agreement.

In respect of the item(s) to be capitalised, complete the table below. Use the DD/MM/YY format for any dates. Show your numeric answers to TWO decimal places.

Leave any unused rows blank.

Details	Acquisition date	Cost £	Funding method
▼			▼
▼			▼

Picklist:

Cash
Finance lease
HF405
Hire purchase
Loan
Part-exchange
PN2948

....

Task 3.5

A business has a policy of capitalising expenditure over £500. The business is not registered for VAT. The standard rate of VAT is 20%.

A business acquires a machine at a cost of £16,000, excluding VAT. This was paid from the bank.

Show the journal to record the acquisition of the machine.

Account	Debit £	Credit £
▼		
▼		

Picklist:

Bank
Machine at cost
Profit or loss account

....

Task 3.6

A business has a policy of capitalising expenditure over £500. The business is registered for VAT.

A machine was purchased for £13,500 excluding VAT. It was paid for by cheque.

Entries have already been made in the accounting records for existing items.

Make the entries in the accounts below to record the acquisition of the machine. On each account, show clearly the balance to be carried down.

Machine at cost

	£			£
Balance b/d	24,500		▼	
	▼		▼	

Bank

	£			£
Balance b/d	32,000		▼	
	▼		▼	
	▼		▼	

VAT control account

	£			£
	▼	Balance b/d		5,000
	▼		▼	

Picklist:

Balance c/d
Bank
Machine at cost
Profit or loss account
VAT control account

22

Task 3.7

Which ONE of the following best explains what is meant by 'capital expenditure'?

Capital expenditure is expenditure:

	✓
On non-current assets, including repairs and maintenance	
On expensive assets	
Relating to the acquisition or improvement of non-current assets	

Task 3.8

Select the terms which correctly reflect the descriptions.

Description	Term
Expenditure for the trade of the business or to repair, maintain and service non-current assets.	▼
Expenditure for the acquisition, replacement or improvement of non-current assets.	▼

Picklist:

Capital expenditure
Revenue expenditure

Task 3.9

A business has a policy of capitalising expenditure over £300. The business's year end is 30 June 20X7.

On 1 July 20X6, the business buys a new property for £500,000 on which it has to pay stamp duty of £15,000. The business also pays the conveyancing solicitor £2,300 for his work on the property purchase.

On 31 December 20X6, the business has to carry out some repairs on the property at a cost of £8,700.

You may ignore VAT in this task.

The business will credit the bank general ledger account for the £526,000 spent on the year.

Ignoring depreciation, what is the impact of recording the debit side of the above transactions on the business's statement of financial position and statement of profit or loss for the year ended 30 June 20X7?

Description	Impact	Amount £
Statement of financial position	▼	
Statement of profit or loss	▼	

Picklist:

Increase current assets
Increase current liabilities
Increase non-current assets
Increase non-current liabilities
Increase profit
No impact
Reduce profit

....

Task 3.10

Complete the following sentences.

It is important to obtain prior authority for capital expenditure in order to ensure that:

	▼

The business's solicitor | ▼ | be the most

appropriate person to give this authority.

Picklist:

the assets are necessary to the business and are purchased at the best price
the assets are recorded in the non-current assets register
the assets are recorded in the general ledger

would
would not

....

Task 3.11

A business is looking to buy a non-current asset for £100,000. The business currently has a positive cash balance of £750. It wishes to become the legal owner of the asset with immediate effect from the date of purchase.

Which would be the most appropriate funding method for this business to purchase this new non-current asset?

	✓
Bank loan	
Cash purchase	
Finance lease	
Hire purchase	

Task 3.12

A business takes out a bank loan for £10,000 in order the finance the purchase of a motor vehicle. The business then purchases the motor vehicle for £9,800.

You may ignore VAT in this task.

Show the journal to record the receipt of the bank loan.

Account	Amount £	Debit ✓	Credit ✓
▼			
▼			

Show the journal to record the purchase of the motor vehicle.

Account	Amount £	Debit ✓	Credit ✓
▼			
▼			

Picklist:

Bank
Finance lease liability
Hire purchase liability
Loan
Motor vehicles accumulated depreciation
Motor vehicles at cost
Motor vehicles running expenses
Purchases ledger control account

Chapter 4 – Depreciation of non-current assets

Task 4.1

What is the purpose of accounting for depreciation in financial statements?

	✓
To spread the cost of a non-current asset over its useful life in order to match the cost of the asset with the consumption of the asset's economic benefits	
To ensure that funds are available for the eventual replacement of the asset	
To reduce the cost of the asset to its estimated market value	
To recognise the fact that assets lose their value over time	

Task 4.2

Complete the following sentence.

Depreciation is an application of the [▼] basis of accounting.

Picklist:

accruals
capital
cash
revenue

Task 4.3

A business has a policy of capitalising expenditure over £500. You may ignore VAT in this task.

Machines are depreciated on a straight line basis. A full year's depreciation is applied in the year of acquisition.

For each non-current asset, for the year ended 31 December 20X8, calculate the:

- **Depreciation charge**
- **Carrying amount of each asset**

(a) Machine purchased for £17,400 on 1 January 20X6 with a useful life of five years and no residual value

Depreciation charge £	Carrying amount £

(b) Machine purchased for £12,800 on 1 January 20X7 with a useful life of four years and a residual value of £2,000

Depreciation charge £	Carrying amount £

(c) Machine purchased for £4,600 on 1 January 20X8 with a useful life of three years and an a residual value of £700

Depreciation charge £	Carrying amount £

Task 4.4

A business has a policy of capitalising expenditure over £500. You may ignore VAT in this task.

Motor vehicles are depreciated on a diminishing balance basis. A full year's depreciation is applied in the year of acquisition.

For each non-current asset, for the year ended 31 March 20X9, calculate the:

- **Depreciation charge**
- **Carrying amount of each asset**

(a) Motor vehicle costing £24,600 purchased on 1 April 20X8 which is to be depreciated at 20% on the diminishing balance basis

Depreciation charge £	Carrying amount £

(b) **Motor vehicle costing £3,800 purchased on 1 November 20X7 which is to be depreciated at 20% on the diminishing balance basis**

Depreciation charge £	Carrying amount £

Task 4.5

A business has a policy of capitalising expenditure over £500. You may ignore VAT in this task.

Motor vehicles are depreciated on a diminishing balance basis. A full year's depreciation is applied in the year of acquisition.

For each non-current asset, for the year ended 31 March 20X9, calculate the:

- **Depreciation charge**
- **Accumulated depreciation**

(a) **Motor vehicle costing £24,000 purchased on 1 April 20X8 which is to be depreciated at 30% on the diminishing balance basis**

Depreciation charge £	Accumulated depreciation £

(b) **Motor vehicle costing £18,700 purchased on 1 August 20X7 which is to be depreciated at 30% on the diminishing balance basis**

Depreciation charge £	Accumulated depreciation £

Task 4.6

A business has a policy of capitalising expenditure over £500. You may ignore VAT in this task.

Computer equipment is depreciated on straight line basis assuming no residual value. Depreciation is calculated on an annual basis and charged in equal instalments for each full month an asset is owned in the year.

For each non-current asset, for the year ended 31 December 20X8, calculate the:

- **Depreciation charge**
- **Carrying amount of each asset**

(a) **Machine purchased on 1 May 20X8 for £15,000. This is to be depreciated at the rate of 20% per annum on the straight line basis**

Depreciation charge £	Carrying amount £

(b) **Computer purchased on 31 October 20X8 for £4,200. This is to be depreciated at the rate of 40% per annum on the straight line basis**

Depreciation charge £	Carrying amount £

Task 4.7

A manufacturing company purchased a new item of plant and machinery for £120,000. The expected number of units to be produced over its useful economic life is 300,000.

Over the last three years it has produced the number of units shown below.

In respect of the asset, calculate the carrying amount b/d, the depreciation charges, the accumulated depreciation, and the carrying amount c/d for the first three years.

Year	Number of units produced	Carrying amount b/d £	Depreciation charges £	Accumulated depreciation £	Carrying amount c/d £
1	90,000				
2	72,000				
3	30,000				

Task 4.8

What is the double entry to record depreciation charges on vehicles in the accounts?

Account	
Debit	▼
Credit	▼

Picklist:

Bank
Depreciation charges
Profit or loss account
Vehicles at cost
Vehicles accumulated depreciation

Task 4.9

A business has a policy of capitalising expenditure over £500. You may ignore VAT in this task.

- You are working on the accounting records of a business for the year ended 31 December 20X5.

- A new vehicle was acquired on 1 April 20X5. It is estimated it will be used for four years.

- The cost was £8,200; this was paid from the bank.

- The business plans to sell the vehicle after four years when its residual value is expected to be £2,000.

- Vehicles are depreciated on a straight line basis. A full year's depreciation is applied in the year of acquisition.

- Entries have already been made in the accounting records for existing items.

Make entries in the accounts below for:

- **The acquisition of the new vehicle**
- **The depreciation charges on the new vehicle**

On each account, show clearly the balance to be carried down or transferred to the profit or loss account, as appropriate.

Vehicles at cost

	£		£
Balance b/d	50,600	▼	
▼		▼	

Depreciation charges

	£		£
Balance b/d	12,300	▼	
▼		▼	

Vehicles accumulated depreciation

	£		£
▼		Balance b/d	24,400
▼			▼

Picklist:

Balance c/d
Bank
Depreciation charges
Profit or loss account
Vehicles accumulated depreciation
Vehicles at cost

Task 4.10

A business buys a machine. The business expects the units of production to vary year on year according to demand for the inventory that the machine will make.

(a) **Which would be the most appropriate depreciation method?**

Depreciation method	✓
Diminishing balance method	
Straight line method	
Units of production method	

The business buys a new table for its office. The business expects the asset's economic benefits to be consumed evenly over 10 years.

(b) **Which would be the most appropriate depreciation method?**

Depreciation method	✓
Diminishing balance method	
Straight line method	
Units of production method	

The business then purchases a computer. The computer is expected to slow down and become less efficient as it ages.

(c)   Which would be the most appropriate depreciation method?

Depreciation method	✓
Diminishing balance method	
Straight line method	
Units of production method	

Task 4.11

A business buys a property with an expected useful life of 50 years. The business wishes to apply the straight line method of depreciation.

What is the appropriate percentage to apply and what should the percentage be applied to?

Percentage: [   ] %

Apply to: [▼]

Picklist:

Accumulated depreciation
Carrying amount
Cost

Chapter 5 – Disposal of non-current assets

Task 5.1

A business has a policy of capitalising expenditure over £500. You may ignore VAT in this task.

- You are working on the accounting records of a business for the year ended 31 March 20X9.

- A machine was acquired on 1 April 20X6.

- The cost was £12,500; this was paid from the bank.

- Machines are depreciated at 30% per annum on the diminishing balance basis, with a full year's charge in the year of acquisition and none in the year of disposal.

- On 30 September 20X8 the asset was sold for £6,000.

Calculate the gain or loss on disposal of the machine. Place a tick in the relevant box to denote whether the amount is a gain or a loss.

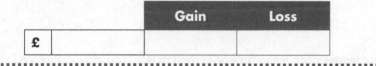

	Gain	Loss
£		

Task 5.2

This task is about the disposal of non-current assets. You may ignore VAT in this task.

- You are working on the accounting records of a business for the year ended 31 March 20X7.

- A motor vehicle was purchased on 1 October 20X4 for £13,800.

- It is being depreciated on the diminishing balance basis at a rate of 40% per annum.

- It was sold on 30 June 20X6 for £5,100.

- A full year's depreciation is applied in the year of acquisition and none in the year of disposal.

Calculate the gain or loss on disposal of the vehicle. Place a tick in the relevant box to denote whether the amount is a gain or a loss.

	Gain	Loss
£		

Task 5.3

Complete the following sentences.

	Answer
The gain or loss arising on disposal of a non-current asset is recorded in the	▼
In the business's accounts, the carrying amount of non-current assets is entered in the	▼
The carrying amount of a non-current asset is calculated as the cost of the asset less the	▼

Picklist:

accumulated depreciation
statement of financial position
statement of profit or loss

....

Task 5.4

This task is about ledger accounting for non-current assets. You may ignore VAT in this task.

- You are working on the accounting records of a business for the year ended 31 December 20X5.

- A machine was acquired on 1 January 20X3. It is estimated it will be used for five years.

- The cost was £25,000.

- Machines are depreciated on a straight line basis assuming no residual value. A full year's depreciation is applied in the year of acquisition and none in the year of disposal.

- The asset was sold on 31 December 20X5 for £12,000.

(a) **Calculate the accumulated depreciation for this asset at 31 December 20X4.**

£	

(b) **For the year ended 31 December 20X5, make entries in the accounts below to reflect the disposal of the machine.**

On each account, show clearly the balance to be carried down or transferred to the statement of profit or loss, as appropriate.

Machine at cost

	£			£
Balance b/d	60,000		▼	
▼			▼	

Bank

	£			£
Balance b/d	22,000		▼	
▼			▼	

Machine accumulated depreciation

	£			£
▼		Balance b/d		26,000
▼			▼	

Disposals

	£			£
▼			▼	
▼			▼	
▼			▼	

Balance c/d
Bank
Depreciation charges
Disposals
Machine accumulated depreciation
Machine at cost
Profit or loss account

(c) **Has the business made a gain or loss on disposal of the machine?**

The business has made a [▼] on disposal of the machine.

Picklist:

gain
loss

Task 5.5

A business sold an item of office equipment which originally cost £20,000. The proceeds of £4,500 were paid into the bank:

(a) **Show the journal entries to record the proceeds.**

Account		Amount £	Debit ✓	Credit ✓
	▼			
	▼			

Picklist:

Bank
Disposals
Office equipment at cost

(b) **Show the journal entries required to remove the original cost of the equipment from the general ledger.**

Account		Amount £	Debit	Credit
	▼			
	▼			

Picklist:

Bank
Depreciation charges
Disposals
Office equipment accumulated depreciation
Office equipment at cost
Profit and loss account

....

Task 5.6

This task is about ledger accounting for non-current assets.

- You are working on the accounting records of a business for the year ended 31 December 20X8.

- A machine was purchased on 1 July 20X6 for £15,600.

- The depreciation policy is to depreciate machines at a rate of 25% per annum on a straight line basis.

- Depreciation is calculated on an annual basis and charged in equal instalments for each full month an asset is owned in the year.

- On 30 November 20X8 the machine was sold for £6,000.

For the year ended 31 December 20X8, make entries in the account below to reflect the disposal of the machine.

Show clearly the balance to be transferred to the statement of profit or loss.

Disposal account

	£			£
▼			▼	
▼			▼	
▼			▼	

Picklist:

Bank
Depreciation charges
Machine accumulated depreciation
Machine at cost
Profit or loss account

....

Task 5.7

Most businesses maintain a non-current assets register.

Which of the following statements best describes the purpose of the non-current assets register?

Select ONE.

	✓
To record non-current assets in the general ledger	
To assist in the physical verification of non-current assets and check the accuracy of the general ledger entries relating to tangible non-current assets	
To list all intangible non-current assets of the business	
To authorise capital expenditure	

Task 5.8

You are working on the accounting records of a business known as LKJ Trading.

LKJ Trading is registered for VAT and has a financial year end of 30 June.

The following is an extract from a purchase invoice received by LKJ Trading:

To: LKJ Trading Unit 6, West End Trading Estate Northgate NG15 6SR	SWF Trading Ltd Stonham Way Whitford WH4 2PO		Date: 01 April 20X6 Invoice 54687
Description	**Item number**	**Quantity**	**£**
Plant	PM672	1	3,000.00
Testing – customer premises	For PM672	1	300.00
Maintenance contract – 24 months	For PM672	1	550.00
Net total			3,850.00
VAT at 20%			770.00
Total			4,620.00

The acquisition has been paid for from the business's bank account.

- LKJ Trading has a policy of capitalising expenditure over £400.
- Plant is depreciated over five years on a straight line basis assuming no residual value.
- Depreciation is calculated on an annual basis and charged in equal instalments for each month the asset is owned.

For the year ended 30 June 20X6, record the following in the extract from the non-current assets register below:

- **The acquisition of the new plant purchased in the year**
- **The depreciation charge on the new plant**
- **The carrying amount**

Show your numerical answers to TWO decimal places

Use the DD/MM/YY format for any dates.

Note. Not every cell will require an entry.

Extract from non-current assets register

Description	Acquisition date	Cost £	Depreciation charges £	Carrying amount £	Funding method	Disposal proceeds £	Disposal date
Plant and machinery							
▼					▼		
Year end 30/06/X6							

Picklist for description:

Accumulated depreciation
Bank
Depreciation charges
Office equipment OF218
Plant PM672

Picklist for funding method:

Cash
Finance lease
Hire purchase
Loan
Part exchange

Task 5.9

You are working on the accounting records of a business known as AM Trading.

You may ignore VAT in this task.

The following information relates to the sale of an item of office equipment no longer used by the business:

Item description	Head office desk DSK452
Date of sale	30 September 20X7
Selling price	£800.00

- AM Trading has a policy of capitalising expenditure over £500.00.

- Office equipment is depreciated at 25% per year on a diminishing balance basis.

- A full year's depreciation is charged in the year of acquisition and none in the year of disposal.

For the year ended 31 December 20X7, update the extract from the non-current assets register for the disposal of the head office desk. Record the:

- **Depreciation charges**
- **Carrying amount**
- **Disposal proceeds**
- **Disposal date**

Show your numerical answers to TWO decimal places.

Use the DD/MM/YY format for any dates.

Note. Not every cell will require an entry.

Extract from the non-current assets register

Description	Acquisition date	Cost £	Depreciation charges £	Carrying amount £	Funding method	Disposal proceeds £	Disposal date
Office equipment							
Desk DSK452	01/06/X5	2,500.00			Loan		
Year end 31/12/X5			625.00	1,875.00			
Year end 31/12/X6			468.75	1,406.25			
Year end 31/12/X7			▼	▼			

Picklist for depreciation charges:

0.00
87.89
351.56

Picklist for carrying amount:

0.00
1,054.69
1,318.36

. . . .

Task 5.10

You are working on the accounting records of a business known as Grimmett.

You may ignore VAT in this task.

Grimmett purchased a computer on 1 April 20X1 for £5,700 (reference COM987).

The current year end is 31 March 20X4.

- Grimmett has a policy of capitalising expenditure over £1,000.

- Grimmett depreciates computers at 20% per year on a straight line basis.

- Depreciation is calculated on an annual basis and charged in equal instalments for each full month the asset is owned in the year.

- On 1 January 20X4, Grimmett sold the computer for £1,300.

For the year ended 31 March 20X4, update the extract from the non-current assets register for the disposal of the computer. Record the:

- Depreciation charges
- Carrying amount
- Disposal proceeds
- Disposal date

Show your numerical answers to TWO decimal places.

Use the DD/MM/YY format for any dates.

Note. Not every cell will require an entry.

Extract from the non-current assets register

Description	Acquisition date	Cost £	Depreciation charges £	Carrying amount £	Funding method	Disposal proceeds £	Disposal date
Office equipment							
Computer COM987	01/04/X1	5,700.00			Part exchange		
Year end 31/03/X2			1,140.00	4,560.00			
Year end 31/03/X3			1,140.00	3,420.00			
Year end 31/03/X4			▼	▼			

Picklist for depreciation charges:

0.00
855.00
1,140.00

Picklist for carrying amount:

0.00
2,565.00
3,135.00

Task 5.11

This task is about the non-current assets register for a business known as CDE Trading. CDE Trading has a financial year end of 31 March.

The following is a purchase invoice received by CDE Trading relating to some items to be used in its office:

To: CDE Trading Unit 6, East End Trading Estate Southgrove HS14 6PW	Refurb & Co 82 Maryland Street Bishops Moat SH34 9TT		Date: 24 June 20 X6 Invoice RE2391
Item	**Details**	**Quantity**	**£**
Refurbished operator chairs	3 × Ergo 803 and 3 × Ergo 697 @ £60 each	6	360.00
Oak boardroom table	2 metres × 1 metre	1	850.00
Delivery and assembly of oak table		1	75.00
Oak maintenance and repair kit		1	60.00
Total			1,345.00
Delivery date: 24/06/X6			

CDE Trading paid the invoice in full on 31 July 20X6 using a £1,345.00 bank loan.

This amount is to be repaid over 12 months.

The following information relates to the sale of a motor vehicle no longer required by the business:

Description	1.6 litre car – AF05 LKR
Date of sale	23 September 20X6
Selling price	£5,340.00

- VAT can be ignored.

- CDE Trading has a policy of capitalising expenditure over £350.

- Furniture and fittings are depreciated at 15% per year on a straight line basis assuming no residual value.

- Motor vehicles are depreciated at 25% per year on a diminishing balance basis.
- A full year's depreciation is applied in the year of acquisition and none in the year of disposal.

For the year ended 31 March 20X7, record the following in the extract from the non-current assets register below:

- **Any acquisitions of non-current assets**
- **Any disposals of non-current assets**
- **Depreciation**

Show your answers to 2 decimal places.

Use the DD/MM/YY format for any dates.

Note. **Not every cell will require an entry, and not all cells will accept entries.**

Extract from non-current assets register

Description/ Serial number	Acquisition date	Cost £	Depreciation charges £	Carrying amount £	Funding method	Disposal proceeds £	Disposal date
Furniture and fittings							
Filling racks	31/10/X5	832.60			Cash		
Year end 31/03/X6			124.89	707.71			
Year end 31/03/X7							
▼					▼		
Year end 31/03/X7							
Motor vehicles							
1.6 litre car AF05 LKR	01/09/X4	10,600.00			Part-exchange		
Year end 31/03/X5			2,650.00	7,950.00			
Year end 31/03/X6			1,987.50	5,962.50			
Year end 31/03/X7			▼	▼			

Description/ Serial number	Acquisition date	Cost £	Depreciation charges £	Carrying amount £	Funding method	Disposal proceeds £	Disposal date
1.8 litre van AD05 ACT	01/09/X5	10,400.00			Part-exchange		
Year end 31/03/X5			2,600.00	7,800.00			
Year end 31/03/X6			1,950.00	5,850.00			
Year end 31/03/X7							

Picklist for description:

1.6 litre car AF05 LKR
1.8 litre van AD05 ACT
Boardroom table and chairs
Oak boardroom table

Picklist for funding method:

Cash
Part-exchange and cash
Loan

Picklist for depreciation charge:

0.00
496.88
1,490.63
1,987.50

Picklist for carrying amount:

0.00
3,975.00
4,471.87
5,465.62

Task 5.12

This task is about the non-current assets register for a business known as QW Trading. QW Trading is registered for VAT and has a financial year end of 31 March.

The following is a purchase invoice received by QW Trading relating to some items to be used in its factory:

To: QW Trading Unit 6, East End Trading Estate Southgrove HS14 6PW	PX Trading Ltd Watchet Way Marston BT23 4RR	Date: 01 April X6 Invoice 23953 VAT 203 9613 01GB £		
Power lathe PM892	Delivery 01 April X6	1		9,930.00
Maintenance contract – 24 months	01/04/X6 – 31/03/X8	1		625.00
Testing – customer premises	2 hrs @ £129.90	2		259.80
Net total				10,814.80
VAT @ 20%				2,162.96
Total				12,977.76

This invoice is to be settled by a hire purchase agreement.
10% deposit is due on the delivery date.

The following information relates to the sale of an item of office equipment no longer needed by the business:

Item description	Reception desk – FaradyR
Date of sale	30 September 20X6
Selling price excluding VAT	£600.00

- QW Trading has a policy of capitalising expenditure over £1,000.

- Machinery is depreciated at 25% per year on a diminishing balance basis.

- Office equipment is depreciated over eight years on a straight line basis assuming no residual value.

- Depreciation is calculated on an annual basis and charged in equal instalments for each full month an asset is owned in the year.

For the year ended 31 March 20X7, record the following in the extract from the non-current assets register:

- **Any acquisitions of non-current assets**
- **Any disposals of non-current assets**
- **Depreciation**

Show your answers to TWO decimal places.

Use the DD/MM/YY format for any dates.

Note. **Not every cell will require an entry, and not all cells will accept entries.**

Extract from non-current assets register

Description/ Serial number	Acquisition date	Cost £	Depreciation charges £	Carrying amount £	Funding method	Disposal Proceeds £	Disposal date
Office equipment							
Copier 4	01/04/X5	3,200.00			Finance lease		
Year end 31/03/X6			400.00	2,800.00			
Year end 31/03/X7							
Reception desk – FaradyR	01/01/X5	1,200.00			Cash		
Year end 31/03/X5			37.50	1,162.50			
Year end 31/03/X6			150.00	1,012.50			
Year end 31/03/X7			▼	▼			

Description/ Serial number	Acquisition date	Cost £	Depreciation charges £	Carrying amount £	Funding method	Disposal Proceeds £	Disposal date
Machinery							
CNC machine CNC3491	01/04/X4	16,400.00			Part-exchange		
Year end 31/03/X5			4,100.00	12,300.00			
Year end 31/03/X6			3,075.00	9,225.00			
Year end 31/03/X7							
▼					▼		
Year end 31/03/X7							

Picklist for description:

CNC Machine CNC 3491
Power lathe PM892
Reception desk – FaradyR
Copier 4

Picklist for depreciation charge:

0.00
75.00
112.50
150.00

Picklist for carrying amount:

0.00
862.50
900.00
937.50

Picklist for funding method:

Cash
Hire purchase
Part-exchange

··

Task 5.13

This task is about ledger accounting for non-current assets.

You are working on the accounts of a business which is not registered for VAT. The business's year end is 31 July 20X6.

- An item of machinery was part exchanged for a newer model on 1 August 20X5.

- The original machinery cost £3,500 on 1 January 20X3.

- The business's depreciation policy for machinery is 15% using the diminishing balance method.

- A full year's depreciation is applied in the year of acquisition and none in the year of disposal.

- A part exchange allowance of £575 was given.

- £2,150 was paid from the bank to complete the purchase of the new machine.

(a) **Complete the following tasks relating to the original item of machinery:**

   (i) **Calculate the accumulated depreciation (to the nearest whole £).**

£	

   (ii) **Complete the disposals account. Show clearly the balance to be carried down or transferred to the statement of profit or loss, as appropriate.**

   Disposals

	£			£
▼			▼	
▼			▼	
▼			▼	

   Picklist:

   Bank
   Machinery accumulated depreciation
   Machinery at cost
   Profit or loss account

(b) **Complete the tasks below:**

(i) **Calculate the total cost of the new machinery from the information above.**

£

Before the part-exchange entries were posted, the balance on the machinery at cost account was £25,820.

The entries have now been correctly made.

(ii) **Complete the sentence:**

The machinery at cost account will have a final balance carried down

of £ when the ledger accounts are closed

for the year.

52

Chapter 6 – Accruals and prepayments

Task 6.1

This task is about ledger accounting for accruals and prepayments.

- During the year ended 31 March 20X6, a business has paid £845 of telephone bills.

- The bill for February and March 20X6 has not been received as at the year end but it is expected to be approximately £170.

Business policy: accounting accruals and prepayments

An entry is made into the income or expense account and an opposite entry into the relevant asset or liability account. In the following period, this entry is removed.

(a) **Write up the following ledger account to reflect the telephone expenses for the year showing the transfer to the statement of profit or loss for the year.**

Telephone expenses

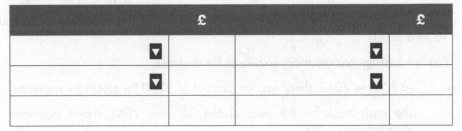

	£		£
▼		▼	
▼		▼	

Picklist:

Accrued expenses
Accrued income
Balance b/d
Balance c/d
Bank
Prepaid expenses
Prepaid income
Profit or loss account
Statement of financial position

At the beginning of the next accounting period the accrual for telephone expenses will need to be reversed.

(b) **Complete the following statements:**

The reversal of this accrual is dated [▼] .

The reversal is on the [▼] side of the telephone expenses account.

Picklist:

31 March 20X6
1 April 20X6
1 April 20X7

credit
debit

Task 6.2

This task is about ledger accounting for accruals and prepayments.

You are working on the accounting records of a business for the year ended 30 June 20X1.

You are looking into electricity expenses for the year.

- At 30 June 20X0, there was an accrual of £370 for electricity expenses.

- The cash book for the year ended 30 June 20X1 shows payments for electricity of £2,300.

- An invoice for £900 for electricity for the period of 1 May 20X1 to 31 July 20X1 was received and paid on 10 August 20X1.

Update the electricity expense and accrued expenses ledger accounts. Show clearly:

- **The reversal of the opening accrual**

- **The cash book figure**

- **The year end adjustment**

- **The balance carried down or the transfer to the statement of profit or loss for the year as appropriate**

Electricity expense (SPL)

	£		£
▼		▼	
▼		▼	

Accrued expenses (SOFP)

	£		£
▼		Balance b/d	370
▼		▼	

Picklist:

Accrued expenses
Accrued expenses (reversal)
Accrued income
Accrued income (reversal)
Balance b/d
Balance c/d
Bank
Electricity expense
Prepaid expenses
Prepaid expenses (reversal)
Prepaid income
Prepaid income (reversal)
Profit or loss account
Statement of financial position

BPP LEARNING MEDIA

Task 6.3

This task is about ledger accounting for accruals and prepayments.

You are working on the accounting records of a business for the year ended 31 May 20X8.

You are looking into insurance expenses for the year.

- There was a prepayment for insurance of £180 at 31 May 20X7.
- The cash book – credit side shows that in the year ended 31 May 20X8 £2,300 was paid for insurance.
- However this includes £250 for the year ending 31 May 20X9.

Update the insurance expense account for the year ended 31 May 20X8. Show clearly:

- **The reversal of the opening prepayment**
- **The cash book figure**
- **The year end adjustment**
- **The transfer to the statement of profit or loss for the year**

Insurance expense

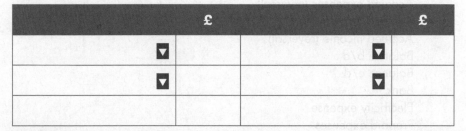

	£		£
▼		▼	
▼		▼	

Picklist:

Accrued expenses
Accrued expenses (reversal)
Accrued income
Accrued income (reversal)
Balance b/d
Balance c/d
Bank
Prepaid expenses
Prepaid expenses (reversal)
Prepaid income
Prepaid income (reversal)
Profit or loss account

Task 6.4

This task is about ledger accounting for accruals and prepayments.

You are working on the accounting records of a business for the year ended 30 June 20X5.

You are looking into rent expenses for the year.

- At 30 June 20X4, there was a prepayment for rent expenses of £300.
- The cash book for the year shows payments for rent of £4,500.
- This amount includes £800 for the 6 months ended 30 September 20X5.

Update the prepaid expenses account. Show clearly:

- **The reversal of the opening prepayment**
- **The year end adjustment**
- **The balance carried down**

Prepaid expenses

	£		£
Balance b/d	300	▼	
▼		▼	

Picklist:

Accrued expenses
Accrued expenses (reversal)
Accrued income
Accrued income (reversal)
Balance b/d
Balance c/d
Bank
Prepaid expenses
Prepaid expenses (reversal)
Prepaid income
Prepaid income (reversal)
Profit or loss account
Rent expense
Rental income

Task 6.5

This task is about accounting for accruals and prepayments.

You are working on the accounting records of a business for the year ended 30 June 20X3.

You are looking into rental income for the year.

- There is accrued rental income of £490 at 30 June 20X2.

- The cash book for the year shows receipts in respect of rental income of £5,600.

- On 10 September 20X3, rental income of £1,500 for the period 1 June 20X3 to 31 August 20X3 was received into the bank.

(a) Calculate the rental income for the year ended 30 June 20X3.

£	

Your junior colleague asks you why you are considering the receipt dated 10 September 20X3.

They are confused as the financial year ended on 30 June 20X3.

(b) Which of the following can you use in your explanation to them?

You must choose ONE answer for each row.

Reason for considering the receipt dated 10 September 20X3	Acceptable reason ✓	Not acceptable reason ✓
The accruals concept requires income to be recorded in the financial statements in the period in which it is earned.		
The proprietor of the business has asked you to increase the profit for the year to maximise his chances of increasing the business' overdraft limit.		
The transaction results in a current liability at 30 June 20X3.		

Task 6.6

An accrual for electricity expenses of £375 was treated as a prepayment in preparing a business's statement of profit or loss for the year ended 31 December 20X4.

What was the resulting effect on the electricity expense of the business for the year? Select ONE.

	✓
Overstated by £375	
Overstated by £750	
Understated by £375	
Understated by £750	

Task 6.7

Cleverley Ltd started in business on 1 January 20X0, preparing accounts to 31 December 20X0. The electricity bills received were as follows.

		£
30 April 20X0	For 4 months to 30 April 20X0	7,279.47
31 July 20X0	For 3 months to 31 July 20X0	4,663.80
31 October 20X0	For 3 months to 31 October 20X0	4,117.28
31 January 20X1	For 3 months to 31 January 20X1	6,491.52

What should the electricity charge be for the year ended 31 December 20X0 (show your answer to 2 decimal places)?

£

Task 6.8

At 31 December 20X0 the accounts of a business show accrued rent payable of £250. During 20X1 the business pays rent bills totalling £1,275, including one bill for £375 in respect of the quarter ending 31 January 20X2.

What is the statement of profit or loss charge for the rent expense for the year ended 31 December 20X1?

£	

....

Task 6.9

During the year £5,000 commission income was received. At the beginning of the year the business was owed £1,000 and at the end of the year the business was owed £500.

What was the commission income figure in the year's statement of profit or loss? Select ONE.

	✓
£4,000	
£4,500	
£5,000	
£5,500	

....

Task 6.10

This task is about accounting for accruals and prepayments.

You are working on the accounting records of a business for the year ended 31 December 20X4.

You are looking into maintenance services income for the year.

- At 31 December 20X3, there was prepaid income in relation to maintenance services of £850.

(a) **Show the journal entry to reverse the opening prepaid income.**

Account		Amount £	Debit ✓	Credit ✓
	▼			
	▼			

Picklist:

Accrued expenses
Accrued income
Balance b/d
Balance c/d
Bank
Maintenance services expense
Maintenance services income
Prepaid expenses
Prepaid income
Profit or loss account

• During the year, the cash book included receipts for maintenance services of £12,750.

• This amount includes £3,000 for the year ended 30 June 20X5.

(b) **Update the maintenance services income account for the year ended 31 December 20X4. Show clearly:**

• **The reversal of the opening prepaid income**
• **The cash book figure**
• **The year end adjustment**
• **The transfer to the statement of profit or loss for the year**

Maintenance services income

		£			£
	▼			▼	
	▼			▼	

Picklist:

Accrued expenses
Accrued income
Balance b/d
Balance c/d
Bank
Maintenance services expense
Maintenance services income
Prepaid expenses
Prepaid expenses (reversal)
Prepaid income
Prepaid income (reversal)
Profit or loss account

....

Task 6.11

This task is about ledger accounting, including accruals and prepayments.

You are working on the final accounts of a business for the year ended 31 March 20X6. In this task, you can ignore VAT.

<hr>

Business policy: accounting for accruals and prepayments

An entry is made into the income or expense account and an opposite entry into the relevant asset or liability account. In the following period, this entry is removed.

<hr>

You are looking at service income:

The cash book for the year shows receipts of service income of £1,680. Service income of £185 is still due for March 20X6 at the year end.

(a) **Update the service income account. Show clearly:**

- **The cash book figure**
- **The year end adjustment**
- **The transfer to the statement of profit or loss for the year**

Service income

	£			£
Accrued income (reversal)	210		▼	
▼			▼	

BPP
LEARNING MEDIA

Picklist:

Accrued expenses
Accrued income
Balance b/d
Balance c/d
Bank
Service income
Prepaid expenses
Prepaid income
Profit or loss account
Sales
Sales ledger control account

(b) **Answer the following regarding the accrued income reversal of £210 in the service income account above.**

(i) **How were the elements of the accounting equation affected by this transaction?**
Tick ONE box for each row.

	Increase ✓	Decrease ✓	No change ✓
Assets			
Liabilities			
Equity			

(ii) **Which ONE of the following dates should be entered for this transaction in the ledger account?**

	✓
1 April 20X5	
31 March 20X5	
31 March 20X6	

You are now looking at insurance expenses for the year.

There was an accrual of £78 on 31 March 20X5. This has been reversed.

The cash book for the year shows payments for insurance of £670, including in March 20X6, £15 paid for insurance covering April 20X6.

(c) **Complete the following statement:**

The administration expenses account needs an adjustment for

[▼] of £ [   ] dated [▼]

Picklist:

Description:
Accrued expenses
Insurance expenses
Amount:
£798
£48
Date:
31 March 20X5
1 April 20X6

(d) **Taking into account all the information you have, calculate the insurance expense for the year ended 31 March 20X6.**

£ [   ]

Chapter 7 – Inventories

Task 7.1

A business has 125 units of a product in inventory which cost £24.60 per unit plus £0.50 per unit of delivery costs. These goods can be sold for £25.80 per unit although in order to do this selling costs of £1.00 per unit must be incurred.

(a) **What is the cost of these units?**

£

(b) **What is their net realisable value?**

£

(c) **At what value will the 125 units of the product be included in the extended trial balance?**

£

Task 7.2

Indicate which TWO of the following can be included as part of the cost of inventory in the accounts.

	✓
Selling costs	
Cost of purchase, including delivery	
Storage costs of finished goods	
Costs of conversion, including direct labour	

Task 7.3

In relation to inventory, what is meant by net realisable value?

	✓
The expected selling price of the inventory	
The expected selling price of the inventory less costs to completion and selling costs	
The replacement cost of the inventory	
The market price of the inventory	

Task 7.4

Accounting for inventory is governed by IAS 2 *Inventories*.

Complete the following sentence.

The rule for inventory is that it should be valued at the [▼]

of [▼] and [▼] .

Picklist:

cost
higher
lower
net realisable value

Task 7.5

A business has five lines of inventory.

Complete the table below.

(a) **Show the:**

- **Net realisable value of each line of inventory**
- **Value PER UNIT of each line of the inventory, for accounting purposes**
- **The total value to appear in the business accounts for each line of inventory**

(b) **On the final row, show the total value of inventory lines A to E to be included in the accounts.**

Inventory line	Quantity (units)	Cost £	Selling price £	Selling costs £	Net realisable value £	Value per unit £	Total value £
A	180	12.50	20.40	0.50			
B	240	10.90	12.60	1.80			
C	300	15.40	22.70	1.20			
D	80	16.50	17.80	1.50			
E	130	10.60	18.00	1.00			
Total							

Task 7.6

(a) Match the descriptions to the relevant method of estimating cost by selecting from the picklist.

Description	Method of estimating cost
Under this method a simple average cost can be calculated whereby the cost of all purchases/production during the year is divided by the total number of units purchased.	▼
Under this method it is assumed that the last goods to be purchased/produced will be the first to be sold.	▼
Under this method it is assumed that the first goods purchased/produced will be the first to be sold.	▼

Picklist:

Average cost
First in first out
Last in first out

(b) Answer the following question.

Question	Answer
Is LIFO permitted by International Financial Reporting Standards?	▼

Picklist:

Yes
No

....

Task 7.7

A business has closing inventory of £20,000.

Show the journal entries to record closing inventory in the general ledger.

Account		Debit £	Credit £
	▼		
	▼		

Picklist:

Closing inventory (SOFP)
Closing inventory (SPL)
Opening inventory
Purchases

Task 7.8

In the business accounts, closing inventory is included in both the statement of financial position and the statement of profit or loss.

Select the terms which best reflect the relationship between inventory and the business accounts.

Statement	Term
Closing inventory in the statement of financial position is best described as	▾
Closing inventory in the statement of profit or loss is best described as	▾

Picklist:

a liability
a reduction in expenses
a reduction in income
an asset
an increase in expenses
an increase in income
capital

Task 7.9

Show whether the following statements are true or false.

Statement	True or false
In the statement of profit or loss, carriage inwards must be included within cost of goods sold.	▾
In the statement of profit or loss, carriage outwards must be included within cost of goods sold.	▾

Task 7.10

Show whether the following statements are true or false.

Statement	True or false
The main purpose of an inventory count is to value inventory at the end of the accounting period.	▼
On a regular basis an inventory reconciliation should be performed, comparing the warehouse's record of the quantity of each item held with the actual quantity counted.	▼

Picklist:

True
False

Task 7.11

Complete the following sentence.

Accounting for inventory as a deduction from cost of goods sold in the statement profit or loss is an application of the [▼] basis of accounting.

Picklist:

accruals
cash
international

Task 7.12

A business that is registered for VAT, sells an item of inventory to customers for £12,000 inclusive of VAT.

Included within the selling price is a profit of £4,000.

What is the cost of this item of inventory?

£ [   ]

Chapter 8 – Irrecoverable and doubtful debts

In this chapter, VAT should be ignored (learning outcome 4.2).

Task 8.1

A business has a balance on its sales ledger control account at 31 December 20X1 of £60,000. As part of its year-end procedures, it has reviewed its customer files and realised that one customer, SH, which owes £4,500 has severe financial difficulties and is unlikely to be able to pay its debt.

Show the journal entries to write off the debt in the general ledger.

Account		Debit £	Credit £
	▼		
	▼		

Picklist:

Bank
Irrecoverable debts
Sales
Sales ledger control account

Task 8.2

A business WH has a balance on its sales ledger control account at 31 March 20X2 of £45,000. As part of its year-end procedures, it has reviewed its customer files and realised that one customer, ZX, which owes £6,900 has severe financial difficulties and is unlikely to be able to pay its debt.

(a) Show the journal entries to write off the debt in the general ledger.

Account		Debit £	Credit £
	▼		
	▼		

(b) Update the sales ledger control account and the irrecoverable debts account to record this information.

As appropriate, on each account show clearly the:

- Balance to be carried down; or
- Balance transferred to the profit or loss account.

Sales ledger control account

	£		£
Balance b/d	45,000		

Irrecoverable debts

	£		£

(c) Write up ZX's subsidiary sales ledger account in the books of WH. Record the irrecoverable debt. Total the sales ledger account (you do not need to enter a balance c/d if it comes to zero).

ZX – Sales ledger account

	£		£
Balance b/d	6,900		

Picklist:

Balance b/d
Balance c/d
Bank
Irrecoverable debts
Sales
Sales ledger control account
Profit or loss account

Task 8.3

A business has a balance on its sales ledger control account at 31 December 20X3 of £70,000. In November 20X3, the business unexpectedly receives £9,500 from a customer. This relates to an amount written off in the previous financial period.

Show the journal entries to record the recovery of this irrecoverable debt previously written off in the general ledger.

Account	Debit £	Credit £
▼		
▼		

Picklist:

Bank
Irrecoverable debts
Sales
Sales ledger control account
Profit or loss account

Task 8.4

RN Trading has a balance on its sales ledger control account at 31 August 20X7 of £86,000.

At 31 August 20X6, the allowance for doubtful debts was £1,160. At 31 August 20X7, the allowance for doubtful debts will be 2% of the outstanding trade receivables.

(a) What is the allowance for doubtful debts at 31 August 20X7?

£ [ ]

(b) What is the allowance for doubtful debts – adjustment for the year ended 31 August 20X7? Select whether it results in an increase or decrease in expenses.

£ [ ] [▼]

Picklist:

Increase in expenses
Decrease in expenses

Task 8.5

WP Trading has a balance on its sales ledger control account at 31 December 20X6 of £90,000. Included within this balance is £4,400 of irrecoverable debts to write off and a specific allowance to be made of £1,300.

At 31 December 20X5, the allowance for doubtful debts was £1,600. At 31 December 20X6, the allowance for doubtful debts will be 4% of the outstanding trade receivables.

Update the following accounts to show this information:

- **Sales ledger control account**
- **Irrecoverable debts**
- **Allowance for doubtful debts (SOFP)**
- **Allowance for doubtful debts – adjustments (SPL)**

As appropriate, on each account show clearly the:

- **Balance carried down; or**
- **Balance transferred to the profit or loss account.**

Sales ledger control account

	£		£
Balance b/d	90,000	▼	
▼		▼	

Irrecoverable debts

	£		£
▼		▼	

Allowance for doubtful debts

	£		£
▼		Balance b/d	1,600
▼		▼	

Allowance for doubtful debts – adjustments

	£			£
▼		▼		

Picklist:

Allowance for doubtful debts
Allowance for doubtful debts – adjustments
Balance b/d
Balance c/d
Bank
Irrecoverable debts
Sales ledger control account
Profit or loss account

Task 8.6

GY Trading has a balance on its sales ledger control account at 31 December 20X6 of £200,000. Included within this balance is £16,000 of irrecoverable debts to write off and a specific allowance to be made of £3,000.

At 31 December 20X5, the allowance for doubtful debts was £7,600. At 31 December 20X6, the allowance for doubtful debts will be 2% of the outstanding trade receivables.

Complete the trial balance extract by entering the figures in the correct places.

Trial balance (extract)

	Ledger balance	
Ledger account	Debit £	Credit £
Sales ledger control account		
Irrecoverable debts		
Allowance for doubtful debts		
Allowance for doubtful debts – adjustments		

Task 8.7

An allowance for doubtful debts is an example of which basis of accounting?

	✓
Depreciation	
Inventory	
Accruals	
Prudence	

Chapter 9 – Bank reconciliations

Task 9.1

Complete the following sentences.

	Answer	
A credit balance on the bank statement indicates a		▼
A credit balance on the cash book indicates a		▼

Picklist:

negative cash balance
positive cash balance

· ·

Task 9.2

Complete the following sentences.

A positive cash balance is a ▼ entry in the cash book.

A negative cash balance is shown on the bank statement as a ▼ entry.

Picklist:

debit
credit

· ·

Task 9.3

Murray's Office Supplies' received the following bank statement for July 20X2.

Date 20X2	Details	Paid out £	Paid in £	Balance £	
01 July	Balance b/d			8,751	C
03 July	Counter credit – LKI		2,875	11,626	C
11 July	Cheque 103122	1,100		10,526	C
13 July	Direct debit – Gas	4,895		5,631	C
14 July	BACS ABW		6,351	11,982	C
18 July	Cheque – 103123	158		11,824	C
27 July	Cheque – 103125	7,565		4,259	C
28 July	Counter credit – OKM		8,590	12,849	C
	D = Debit, C = Credit				

(a) **Check the items on the bank statement against the items in the cash book below.**

(b) **Enter any items into the cash book as needed.**

(c) **Total the cash book and clearly show the balance carried down at 31 July AND brought down at 1 August.**

Cash book as at 31 July

Date 20X2	Details	Bank £	Date 20X2	Cheque number	Details	Bank £
01 July	Balance b/d	8,751	11 July	103122	ENG	1,100
03 July	LKI	2,875	18 July	103123	JHP	158
14 July	ABW	6,351	27 July	103125	MWY	7,565
17 July	WNY	3,560	29 July	103126	YMN	4,320

(d) Identify the **TWO** transactions that are included in the cash book but missing from the bank statement and complete the bank reconciliation statement below as at 31 July.

Bank reconciliation statement		£
Balance per bank statement		
	▼	
Total to add		
	▼	
Total to subtract		
Balance as per cash book		

Picklist:

Balance b/d
Balance c/d
ABW
Direct debit – Gas
ENG
JHP
LKI
MWY
OKM
WNY
YMN

Task 9.4

The balance showing on the bank statement is a debit of £778 and the balance in the cash book is a debit of £3,851.

The bank statement has been compared to the cash book and the following differences identified:

(1) Bank charges of £25 are included on the bank statement but have not been entered in the cash book.

(2) Cash receipts totalling £1,738 have been entered in the cash book but are not yet banked.

(3) An automated receipt from a credit customer for £743 has been incorrectly entered in the cash book as £734. It is correct on the bank statement.

(4) A BACS payment of £2,827 has not been entered in the cash book.

(5) A cheque sent to a supplier for £452 has been entered in the cash book but has not yet cleared the bank statement.

(6) The bank made an error and duplicated the payment of a standing order for £500.

Use the following table to show the THREE adjustments you need to make to the cash book.

Adjustment		Amount £	Debit ✓	Credit ✓
	▼			
	▼			
	▼			

Picklist:

Adjustment (1)
Adjustment (2)
Adjustment (3)
Adjustment (4)
Adjustment (5)
Adjustment (6)

Task 9.5

The balance showing on the bank statement is a credit of £7,377 and the balance in the cash book is a debit of £11,442.

The bank statement has been compared to the cash book and the following differences identified:

(1)   A cheque sent to a supplier for £990 has been entered in the cash book but has not yet cleared the bank statement.

(2)   Cash receipts totalling £3,560 have been entered in the cash book but are not yet banked.

(3)   An BACS receipt from a credit customer for £996 has cleared the bank statement but has not yet been entered in the cash book.

(4)   A faster payment of £2,827 for the purchase of a non-current asset has cleared the bank statement but has not been entered in the cash book.

(5)   A cheque sent to a supplier for £776 has been entered in the cash book but has not yet cleared the bank statement.

(6)   Bank charges paid of £440 were not entered in the cash book.

Use the following table to show the THREE adjustments you need to make to the cash book.

Adjustment		Amount £	Debit ✓	Credit ✓
	▼			
	▼			
	▼			

Picklist:

Adjustment (1)
Adjustment (2)
Adjustment (3)
Adjustment (4)
Adjustment (5)
Adjustment (6)

....

Chapter 10 – Control account reconciliations

Task 10.1

Given below are summaries of transactions with receivables for the month of February for a business. The balance on the sales ledger control account at 1 February was £4,268.

	£
Goods sold on credit	15,487
Goods returned by credit customers	995
Irrecoverable debts	210
Money received from credit customers	13,486
Discounts allowed	408
Contra entries	150

Enter the items above in the sales ledger control account (including the balance b/d at the start of the month). Show the balance c/d at the end of the month.

Sales ledger control account

	£		£
▼		▼	
▼		▼	
▼		▼	
▼		▼	
▼		▼	
▼		▼	

Picklist:

Balance b/d
Balance c/d
Bank
Discounts allowed
Irrecoverable debts
Purchases ledger control account
Sales
Sales returns

Task 10.2

The balance on the purchases ledger control account for a business at 1 February was £3,299. The transactions with payables for the month of February are summarised below:

	£
Credit purchases	12,376
Cheques to payables	10,379
Returns to credit suppliers	1,074
Discounts received	302
Contra entry	230

Enter the items above in the purchases ledger control account (including the balance b/d at the start of the month). Show the balance c/d at the end of the month.

Purchases ledger control account

	£		£
▼		▼	
▼		▼	
▼		▼	
▼		▼	
▼		▼	

Picklist:

Balance b/d
Balance c/d
Bank
Discounts received
Purchases
Purchases returns
Sales ledger control account

Task 10.3

At 31 March the balance on a business's sales ledger control account was £7,380 but the total of the list of balances from the sales ledger was £6,310. The following errors were discovered:

(1) A customer account with a credit balance of £460 was omitted from the total of the subsidiary sales ledger account balances.

(2) A contra entry for £250 has been made in the sales ledger control account but not in the subsidiary ledger.

(3) A cash book – debit side total of £1,650 has been posted to the wrong side of the sales ledger control account.

(4) A total of the sales day book has been undercast by £1,000.

(5) A credit note to a customer for £680 has been entered on the wrong side of the customer's account in the sales ledger.

(6) A total of the discounts allowed book of £840 has been omitted from the sales ledger control account.

Use the following table to show the THREE adjustments required to the sales ledger control account.

Adjustment		Amount £	Debit ✓	Credit ✓
	▼			
	▼			
	▼			

Picklist:

Adjustment (1)
Adjustment (2)
Adjustment (3)
Adjustment (4)
Adjustment (5)
Adjustment (6)

Task 10.4

At 31 December the balance on a business's sales ledger control account was £11,840 but the total of the list of balances from the sales ledger was £6,100. The following errors were discovered:

(1) The subsidiary sales ledger account of G Hargreaves was understated by £100.

(2) A total in the sales returns day book was undercast by £3,000.

(3) A total in the sales day book of £2,400 was duplicated in the sales ledger control account.

(4) A sales invoice of £570 was incorrectly posted to the wrong side of the sales ledger account. It was entered correctly in the sales day book.

(5) A credit note to a customer for £680 has been entered on the wrong side of the customer's account in the sales ledger.

(6) A contra entry for £460 has been entered in the subsidiary sales ledger but was not posted to the sales ledger control account.

Use the following table to show the THREE adjustments required to the listing of subsidiary sales ledger balances.

Adjustment		Amount £	Debit ✓	Credit ✓
	▼			
	▼			
	▼			

Picklist:

Adjustment (1)
Adjustment (2)
Adjustment (3)
Adjustment (4)
Adjustment (5)
Adjustment (6)

Task 10.5

The balance on a business's purchases ledger control account at 31 January was £3,450 but the total of the list of balances from the purchases ledger was £2,219 at the same date. The following errors were discovered:

(1)   A credit note of £160 to R Milne was incorrectly entered in the subsidiary ledger account of J Roberts.

(2)   A page in the purchases day book had been overcast by £850.

(3)   A total in the purchases returns day book of £791 was entered in the general ledger as £719.

(4)   A contra entry of £214 was included in the purchases ledger control account but has been omitted from the relevant subsidiary purchases ledger accounts.

(5)   A purchases credit note of £403 was recorded as a credit entry in the purchases ledger. It is correctly entered in the purchases day book.

(6)   A total in the cash book – credit side of £1,329 has been omitted from the purchases ledger control account.

Use the following table to show the adjustments you need to make to the purchases ledger control account.

Adjustment		Amount £	Debit ✓	Credit ✓
	▼			
	▼			
	▼			

Picklist:

Adjustment (1)
Adjustment (2)
Adjustment (3)
Adjustment (4)
Adjustment (5)
Adjustment (6)

Task 10.6

The balance on a business's purchases ledger control account at 31 January was £5,248 but the total of the list of balances from the purchases ledger was £8,670 at the same date. The following errors were discovered:

(1) The total from the discounts received day book of £980 was omitted from the purchases ledger control account.

(2) A page in the purchases day book totalling £3,592 was omitted from the general ledger.

(3) A purchases invoice of £660 was entered on the wrong side of the subsidiary purchases ledger account.

(4) A credit note of £1,210 was omitted from the subsidiary purchases ledger account.

(5) The total of a page in the cash book – credit side relating to payments to suppliers was undercast by £320.

(6) Purchases credit notes totalling £620 had incorrectly been entered on the credit side of the subsidiary purchases ledger account.

Use the following table to show the THREE adjustments required to the listing of subsidiary purchases ledger balances.

Adjustment	Amount £	Debit ✓	Credit ✓
▼			
▼			
▼			

Picklist:

Adjustment (1)
Adjustment (2)
Adjustment (3)
Adjustment (4)
Adjustment (5)
Adjustment (6)

Task 10.7

This task is about period end routines.

You are preparing the reconciliation between a credit supplier's statement of account and the supplier's account as shown in the purchases ledger of Magenta at the end of June 20X6.

Gerry Green
Garden Industrial Estate
Westham WM2 3FS

To: Magenta
14 Manor Road
Eastham
EM3 4NJ

Statement of account

Date 20X6	Details	Transaction amount	Outstanding amount
01 June	Opening balance		500
02 June	Cheque	420	80
10 June	Invoice 147	1,750	1,830
17 June	Credit note 23	530	1,300
22 June	Invoice 178	925	2,225
29 June	Invoice 195	1,250	3,475

Purchases ledger account – Gerry Green

Date 20XX	Details	Amount £	Date 20XX	Details	Amount £
02 June	Cheque	420	01 June	Balance b/f	500
17 June	Purchases returns – credit note 23	530	10 June	Purchases – invoice 147	1,750
			22 June	Purchases – invoice 178	925

(a) **Calculate the balance on the supplier's account in Magenta's purchases ledger and reconcile this with the balance showing on the supplier's statement of account.**

	£
Balance on supplier's statement of account	3,475
Balance on supplier's account in purchases ledger	
Difference	

(b) **Which item on the supplier's statement of account has not yet been entered in the supplier's account in Magenta's purchases ledger?**

Items	✓
Cheque for £420	
Invoice number 147	
Credit note number 23	
Invoice number 178	
Invoice number 195	

Task 10.8

This task is about accounting for payroll.

Marten Trading pays its employees by bank transfer every month and maintains a wages control account (also known as the 'net pay control account'). A summary of last month's payroll transactions is shown below.

Item	Amount £
Gross pay	120,000
Employees' NI	4,000
Income tax	16,000
Employer's NI	8,000

In the general ledger:

(a)   Record the wages expense

Account name	Amount £	Debit ✓	Credit ✓
▼			
▼			

(b)   Record the HM Revenue and Customs liability

Account name	Amount £	Debit ✓	Credit ✓
▼			
▼			

(c)   Record the net wages paid to the employees

Account name	Amount £	Debit ✓	Credit ✓
▼			
▼			

Picklist:

Bank
HM Revenue and Customs
Wages control account
Wages expense

Chapter 11 – The trial balance, errors and the suspense account

Task 11.1

In the 'type of error' column, show the error being described in the 'Description' column.

In the 'balancing trial balance' column, indicate whether the error will permit the trial balance to balance or not.

Description	Type of error	Balancing trial balance
A debit entry has been posted with no corresponding credit made.	▼	▼
An entry has been made so that debits equal credits but the amount is incorrect.	▼	▼
A transaction has been recorded at the correct amount but the debit and credit entries have been reversed.	▼	▼
Debits equal credits; however, one of the entries has been made to the wrong type of account.	▼	▼

Picklist for type of error:

Error of original entry
Error of principle
Reversal of entries
Single entry error

Picklist for balancing trial balance:

No
Yes

Task 11.2

For each of the following errors indicate whether there is an imbalance in the trial balance or not.

Error	Imbalance ✓	No imbalance ✓
The payment of the telephone bill was posted to the cash book – credit side and then credited to the telephone account.		
The depreciation expense was debited to the accumulated depreciation account and credited to the depreciation charges account.		
The electricity account balance of £750 was taken to the trial balance as £570.		
The motor expenses were debited to the motor vehicles at cost account. The credit entry is correct.		
Discounts received were not posted to the general ledger.		

Task 11.3

A trial balance has been prepared for a business and the total of the debit balances is £228,678 and the total of the credits is £220,374.

What is the balance on the suspense account?

	Debit balance ✓	Credit balance ✓
£		

Task 11.4

Show the journal entries required to correct each of the following errors.

Narratives are not required. Ignore VAT.

(a) Telephone expenses of £236 were debited to the electricity account.

Account name		Debit £	Credit £
▼			
▼			

(b) A sales invoice for £645 was entered into the sales day book as £465.

Account name		Debit £	Credit £
▼			
▼			

(c) A credit note received from a supplier for £38 was omitted from the purchases returns day book.

Account name		Debit £	Credit £
▼			
▼			

Picklist:

Electricity
Purchases ledger control account
Purchases returns
Sales
Sales ledger control account
Telephone

Task 11.5

Show the journal entries required to correct each of the following errors.

Narratives are not required. Ignore VAT.

(a) The increase in allowance for doubtful debts of £127 was debited to the allowance for doubtful debts account and credited to the allowance for doubtful debts adjustment account.

Account name		Debit £	Credit £
	▼		
	▼		

(b) A contra entry of £200 was debited to the sales ledger control account and credited to the purchases ledger control account.

Account name		Debit £	Credit £
	▼		
	▼		

(c) The irrecoverable debts expense of £680 was omitted from the general ledger.

Account name		Debit £	Credit £
	▼		
	▼		

Picklist:

Allowance for doubtful debts
Allowance for doubtful debts – adjustments
Irrecoverable debts
Purchases ledger control account
Sales ledger control account

Task 11.6

This task is about accounting adjustments.

You are a trainee accounting technician reporting to a managing partner in an accounting practice. You are working on the accounting records of a business client.

A trial balance has been drawn up and balanced using a suspense account. You now need to make some corrections and adjustments for the year ended 31 December 20X7.

You may ignore VAT in this task.

Depreciation on the plant must be calculated. Plant is depreciated at 20% per year on a straight line basis assuming no residual value.

(a) **Calculate the depreciation charge on plant for the year.**

£	

(b) **(i)** **Record this adjustment into the extract from the extended trial balance below.**

(ii) **Make the following further adjustments.**

You will NOT need to enter adjustments on every line. Do NOT enter zeros into unused cells.

- The carriage outwards balance of £460 was omitted from the trial balance. The corresponding entry (a cheque payment) is correctly included in the cash book.

- The purchases balance was incorrectly transferred to the trial balance. The balance should be £88,540 and not £89,430.

- The payment of office expenses of £70 has been reversed in both general ledger accounts.

Extract from the extended trial balance

Ledger account	Ledger balances		Adjustments	
	Debit £	Credit £	Debit £	Credit £
Bank	5,321			
Carriage outwards				
Depreciation charges				
Irrecoverable debts	632			
Office expenses	52,832			
Plant at cost	32,400			
Plant accumulated depreciation		6,480		
Prepaid expenses	305			
Purchases	89,430			
Purchases ledger control account		11,230		
Rent	12,520			
Sales		104,502		
Sales ledger control account	16,230			
Suspense		430		
VAT		9,320		

Task 11.7

This task is about accounting adjustments.

You are a trainee accounting technician reporting to a managing partner in an accounting practice. You are working on the accounting records of a business client.

A trial balance has been drawn up and balanced using a suspense account. You now need to make some corrections and adjustments for the year ended 30 April 20X9.

You may ignore VAT in this task.

The allowance for doubtful debts needs to be adjusted to 2% of the outstanding trade receivables.

(a) **Calculate the value of the adjustment required.**

£	

(b) **(i)** **Record this adjustment into the extract from the extended trial balance below.**

     (ii) **Make the following further adjustments.**

You will NOT need to enter adjustments on every line. Do NOT enter zeros into unused cells.

- Closing inventory has been valued at £8,430.

- The bank balance has been included on the wrong side of the trial balance.

- Purchases returns of £560 have been correctly included in the purchases ledger control account. The other entry was omitted.

Extract from the extended trial balance

Ledger account	Ledger balances		Adjustments	
	Debit £	Credit £	Debit £	Credit £
Allowance for doubtful debts		350		
Allowance for doubtful debts – adjustments				
Accrued expenses		750		
Bank		6,320		
Carriage inwards	219			
Closing inventory				
Depreciation charges	6,625			
Discounts allowed	620			
Office expenses	488			
Opening inventory	4,420			
Prepaid expenses	305			
Purchases	89,430			
Purchases returns				
Purchases ledger control account		11,230		
Sales		104,502		
Sales ledger control account	18,200			
Suspense	12,080			

BPP LEARNING MEDIA

Task 11.8

You are a trainee accounting technician working in an accounting practice. You are working on the accounting records of a business known as SYH Trading for the year ended 30 September 20X6. The proprietor of SYH Trading is trying to obtain a bank loan for the business and is keen to maximise the profit for the year to encourage the bank to lend. Your line manager is concerned that the proprietor might propose year end adjustments with the deliberate intent of maximising profit. Therefore, she has asked you to look out for period end adjustments which would result in an increase to profit for the year.

Which of the following period end adjustments would result in an increase to profit for the year?

Choose ONE.

	✓
A decrease in the allowance for doubtful debts from 3% of outstanding trade receivables to 2% of outstanding trade receivables	
The write down of an item of inventory which cost £1,500 and had a selling price of £1,350 and expected selling costs of £200	
Recognising an accrual for vehicle running expenses for September 20X6 but not invoiced and paid until October 20X6	
Decreasing the useful life of a computer with effect from the start of the year (1 October 20X5)	

Task 11.9

You are a trainee accounting technician reporting to a managing partner in an accounting practice. You are working on the accounting records of a business known as KSB Trading for the year ended 31 December 20X6. The proprietor is KSB Trading is a great friend of the managing partner in your accounting practice. KSB Trading is trying to increase its bank overdraft limit and a meeting is set up with the bank next week. The proprietor is convinced that the current year's profit should persuade the bank to increase the overdraft limit and has asked the managing partner not to amend the draft profit figure. The managing partner has asked you to respect the proprietor's wishes.

As part of your preparation of the year end accounts, you have discovered a letter from one of KSB Trading's customers explain that they have gone into liquidation and are unable to pay the amount owing to KSB Trading. No adjustment has been made in respect of this.

What should you do next and why?

Choose ONE.

	✓
Complete the accounts without any further adjustment, as any change could affect the outcome of the meeting with the bank.	
Complete the accounts without any further adjustment because the client's needs must take priority.	
Explain to the managing partner that you have discovered an irrecoverable debt which needs writing off because the accounts must be prepared in accordance with International Financial Reporting Standards.	
Write off the irrecoverable debt without telling your managing partner as you want to make sure that you get the pay rise that he's promised you.	

Task 11.10

You are a trainee accounting technician reporting to a managing partner in an accounting practice. You are working on the accounting records of a business known as TWG Trading for the year ended 30 June 20X3. Whilst you are preparing the accounts for the year ended 30 June 20X3, you come across some cash sales recorded on 30 June 20X3 which are then reversed out as sales returns on 1 July 20X3.

What should you do next and why?

Choose ONE.

	✓
Do nothing because the cash sales were accurately recorded in the cash book.	
Seek advice from the managing partner as it is possible that these sales were deliberately created with the intention of increasing profit for the year ended 30 June 20X3 and are not a genuine business transaction.	
Ignore the discovery because the client is a good friend and you trust him implicitly.	
Insist that the client reverses these sales and threaten to resign because it is clear that there has deliberately overstated the profit.	

Task 11.11

Which of the following statements about the trial balance is correct?

Choose ONE.

	✓
It is a memorandum account to keep track of amounts owing from individual customers and owed to individual suppliers.	
It will detect all bookkeeping errors.	
It is prepared after closing off the general ledger accounts and before preparing the final accounts.	
It will always include a suspense account.	

Task 11.12

This task is about accounting adjustments.

You are working as an accounting technician for a sole trader business with a year end of 30 September. A trial balance has been drawn up and a suspense account opened. You now need to make some corrections and adjustments for the year ended 30 September 20X6.

You may ignore VAT for this task.

Record the journal entries needed in the general ledger to deal with the items below.

You should:

- **Remove any incorrect entries where appropriate**
- **Post the correct entries**

Do NOT enter zeros into unused column cells.

Note. **You do NOT need to give narratives.**

(a) **Depreciation of £1,056 on fixtures and fittings has not yet been accounted for.**

Account	Debit £	Credit £
▼		
▼		

Picklist:

Depreciation expense
Fixtures and fittings cost
Fixtures and fittings accumulated depreciation
Suspense

(b) **An accrual for a telephone bill of £120 has been made correctly to the telephone expenses account but the other side of the entry has not been posted.**

Account	Debit £	Credit £
▼		
▼		

Picklist:

Accruals
Telephone expense
Prepayments
Purchases
Suspense

(c) **Closing inventory for the year end 30 September 20X6 has not yet been recorded. Its value at cost is £8,450. Included in this figure are some items costing £445 that will be sold for £250.**

Account		Debit £	Credit £
	▼		
	▼		

Picklist:

Closing inventory – statement of financial position
Closing inventory – statement of profit or loss

(d) **Credit notes of £887 have been posted to the correct side of the purchases ledger control account, but have been made to the same side of the purchases returns account.**

Account		Debit £	Credit £
	▼		
	▼		

Picklist:

Purchase ledger control account
Sales ledger control account
Purchase returns
Suspense
Sales returns

Now that you have posted the journals, you are pleased to see that the suspense account is clear and the trial balance totals agree.

(e) **Complete the following sentences:**

▼

conclude that the balances included are now free from all errors.

▼

conclude that the debt and credit sides of the trial balance will be equal.

Picklist:

I can
I cannot

Chapter 12 – The extended trial balance

Task 12.1

(a) **Complete the following sentence.**

An extended trial balance is an accounting technique of moving from the

[____ ▼] trial balance, through the year end adjustments, to the figures

for the [____ ▼] accounts.

Picklist:

final

initial

(b) **Complete the following sentence.**

When an extended trial balance is extended and a business has made a profit, this figure for profit will be in the [____ ▼] column of the statement of profit or loss.

Picklist:

credit

debit

Task 12.2

In respect of the extended trial balance, show which ONE of the following statements is correct.

Statements	✓
The balance on the suspense account should appear on the debit side of the statement of profit or loss columns.	
The balance on the suspense account should appear on the credit side of the statement of financial position columns.	
The balance on the suspense account should not appear in the statement of profit or loss or the statement of financial position columns in the extended trial balance.	

Task 12.3

Enter a tick in the relevant place to show where the following ledger accounts are usually included in the extended trial balance.

Where necessary, enter more than one tick on a row.

Extended trial balance

Ledger account	Statement of profit or loss		Statement of financial position	
	Debit ✓	Credit ✓	Debit ✓	Credit ✓
Allowance for doubtful debts				
Allowance for doubtful debts – adjustment (increase in allowance)				
Bank overdraft				
Capital				
Closing inventory				
Depreciation charges				
Purchases returns				
Opening inventory				
VAT owed from HMRC				

Task 12.4

Extend the figures into the statement of profit or loss and statement of financial position columns.

Do NOT enter zeros into unused column cells.

Complete the extended trial balance by entering figures and a label in the correct places.

Extended trial balance

Ledger account	Ledger balances		Adjustments		Statement of profit or loss		Statement of financial position	
	Debit £	Credit £	Debit £	Credit £	Debit £	Credit £	Debit £	Credit £
Allowance for doubtful debts		2,380	420					
Allowance for doubtful debts – adjustment	1,600			420				
Bank	2,400			230				
Capital		25,800						
Closing inventory			13,500	13,500				
Depreciation charges	9,203		4,000					
Office expenses	600							
Opening inventory	2,560							
Payroll expenses	16,400							
Purchases	22,400							
Purchases ledger control account		8,900	300					
Sales		45,150		60				
Sales ledger control account	11,205			300				
Selling expenses	1,700							
Suspense	170		60	230				
VAT		12,000						
Vehicles at cost	64,192							
Vehicles accumulated depreciation		38,200		4,000				
▼								
Total	132,430	132,430	18,510	18,510				

Picklist:

Balance b/d
Balance c/d
Gross loss for the year
Gross profit for the year
Loss for the year
Profit for the year
Suspense

....

Task 12.5

Extend the figures into the statement of profit or loss and statement of financial position columns.

Do NOT enter zeros into unused column cells.

Complete the extended trial balance by entering figures and a label in the correct places.

Extended trial balance

Ledger account	Ledger balances		Adjustments		Statement of profit or loss		Statement of financial position	
	Debit £	Credit £	Debit £	Credit £	Debit £	Credit £	Debit £	Credit £
Bank		4,123		4,235				
Capital		20,000						
Closing inventory			3,414	3,414				
Depreciation charges	2,415		1,352					
Irrecoverable debts	124							
Loan		10,000						
Machine at cost	51,600							
Machine accumulated depreciation		13,210		1,352				
Opening inventory	6,116							
Prepaid expenses	215		352					
Purchases	39,321		519					
Purchases ledger control account		13,421						
Purchases returns		299		519				
Sales		72,032		511				
Sales ledger control account	38,597			3,770				
Sales returns	2,057		511					
Suspense		3,418	3,770	352				
VAT		3,942	4,235					
▼								
Total	140,445	140,445	14,153	14,153				

Picklist:

Balance b/d
Balance c/d
Gross loss for the year
Gross profit for the year
Loss for the year
Profit for the year
Suspense

Answer Bank

Answer Bank

Chapter 1

Task 1.1

The sales returns day book lists	credit notes sent to customers
The purchases day book lists	invoices received from suppliers
The purchases returns day book lists	credit notes received from suppliers
The sales day book lists	invoices sent to customers

Explanation:

Remember, the books of prime entry are the records in which transactions are initially recorded. Postings will then be made from the books of prime entry to the ledgers.

....

Task 1.2

(a)

Account	Debit £	Credit £
Bank	15,000	
Capital		15,000

(b)

Account	Debit £	Credit £
Rent	2,000	
Bank		2,000

(c)

Account	Debit £	Credit £
Purchases	6,200	
Bank		6,200

(d)

Account	Debit £	Credit £
Electricity	150	
Bank		150

Explanation:

For every transactions, there is a dual effect on the general ledger (ie a debit entry and a corresponding credit entry).

....

Task 1.3

Bank

	£		£
Capital (1)	20,000	Purchases (2)	2,100
Sales (3)	870	Purchases ledger control account (6)	1,500
Sales ledger control account (7)	1,600	Balance c/d	18,870
	22,470		22,470
Balance b/d	18,870		

Capital

	£		£
Balance c/d	20,000	Bank (1)	20,000
	20,000		20,000
		Balance b/d	20,000

Purchases

	£		£
Bank (2)	2,100	Profit or loss account	4,900
Purchases ledger control account (4)	2,800		
	4,900		4,900

Purchases ledger control account

	£		£
Bank (6)	1,500	Purchases (4)	2,800
Balance c/d	1,300		
	2,800		2,800
		Balance b/d	1,300

Sales

	£		£
Profit or loss account	4,270	Bank (3)	870
		Sales ledger control account (5)	3,400
	4,270		4,270

Sales ledger control account

	£		£
Sales (5)	3,400	Bank (7)	1,600
		Balance c/d	1,800
	3,400		3,400
Balance b/d	1,800		

Explanation:

The statement of financial position accounts (bank, capital, purchases ledger control account and sales ledger control account) are totalled at the period end. For each account a balance c/d and balance b/d is calculated.

The statement of profit or loss accounts (purchases and sales) are totalled at the year end. The balancing figures are taken to the profit or loss account.

....

Task 1.4

Trial balance	Amount £	Debit £	Credit £
Bank (positive balance)	11,000	**11,000**	
Capital	14,000		**14,000**
Electricity	2,000	**2,000**	
Purchases	4,500	**4,500**	
Purchases ledger control account	3,000		**3,000**
Rent expense	2,500	**2,500**	
Sales	9,000		**9,000**
Sales ledger control account	12,000	**12,000**	
VAT control account (due to HMRC)	6,000		**6,000**
		32,000	**32,000**

Explanation:

In accordance with the principles of double entry bookkeeping, assets and expenses are entered on the debit side of the trial balance. Liabilities, income and capital are recorded on the credit side of the trial balance.

....

Task 1.5

(a)

Ledger account	Amount £	Debit ✓	Credit ✓
Sales	13,000		✓
Sales returns	1,000	✓	
Purchases	8,000	✓	
Purchases returns	2,000		✓
Bank	3,500	✓	

(b)

Amount owed at the end of the period: £	2,500
Asset or liability	Liability

Explanation:

The amount owed at the end of the period is calculated as sales £13,000 plus purchases returns £2,000 less sales returns £1,000 less purchases £8,000 less bank £3,500 = £2,500.

The credit entries exceed the debit entries. This shows that there is an amount owed to HMRC at the end of the period, and therefore a liability.

....

Chapter 2

Task 2.1

Description	Term
Assets which do not have a physical substance, for example licences and brands	Intangible assets
Assets which have a physical substance, for example property, plant and equipment	Tangible assets

Task 2.2

Description	Term
This shows what the business owes back to its owner.	Capital
These relate to liabilities owed by the business due to its day-to-day activities and include trade payables, accruals, VAT owed to the tax authorities and bank overdrafts.	Current liabilities
These are costs that a business has incurred over the accounting period.	Expenses
These relate to assets used by the business on a day-to-day basis and include inventory, trade receivables and bank balances.	Current assets
Tangible or intangible assets held and used in the business over the long term (ie more than one year).	Non-current assets
These are amounts that the business has earned over the accounting period.	Income
These relate to the long-term debts of the business and include items such as long-term bank loans.	Non-current liabilities

Task 2.3

Item	Asset, liability, income, expense or capital
A laptop used in the accounts department of a retail store	Asset
Equity interest	Capital
A bank loan	Liability

Explanation:

The classifications reflect the principles of double entry bookkeeping.

....

Task 2.4

	✓
an asset, capital or an expense	
a liability or an expense	
an amount owing to the organisation	
a liability, capital or income	✓

Explanation:

Statement 1: This is incorrect as assets and expenses are debit balances, not credit balances.

Statement 2: This is incorrect as an expense is a debit balance, not a credit balance.

Statement 3: This is incorrect as an amount owing to the organisation is an asset. An asset is a debit balance, not a credit balance.

....

Task 2.5

Scenarios	Fundamental principle
Employees who may receive a bonus depending on the financial performance of the accounting practice do not prepare the accounting practice's financial statements.	Objectivity
The new trainee accounting technician is supervised by her manager and receives the necessary training.	Professional competence and due care

Task 2.6

Control procedures	✓
Physical controls	✓
Segregation of duties	
Authorisation of transactions	
Written record of procedures	

Explanation:

Businesses should ensure physical restrictions are in place to limit access to assets such as inventory.

Task 2.7

	✓
To ensure that the accounting policies selected maximise the business's profits	
To ensure the accounting records truly reflect the transactions and financial results of the business	✓
To ensure that the business acts in the owner's best interests	
To minimise the tax payable on the business's profits	

Explanation:

Accounting policies should result in information that is relevant and reliable to users of financial statements rather than with the aim of maximising the business's profits.

The business should act in the business's and its stakeholders' best interests rather than the owner's own personal interests.

As explained above, accounting policies should be designed around making the information relevant and reliable rather than specifically to minimise the tax liability on the business's profits.

Task 2.8

	✓
Reviews	
Written record of procedures	
Physical controls	✓
Authorisation of transactions	

Explanation:

Physical controls are most appropriate here. The checkout operation and store manager should count the cash float together at the beginning and end of the day and a written record of the amount should be made. The physical cash amount should then be reconciled to the expected amount of cash from the till receipts by the store manager and any discrepancies investigated.

Task 2.9

	Acceptable reason ✓	Not acceptable reason ✓
The business has high value desirable inventory making the risk of theft high which could be covered up by unauthorised alteration of accounting records.	✓	
Only the accounts department are likely to have the necessary skills and knowledge to maintain the accounting records.	✓	
The password will prevent anyone in the accounts department deliberately manipulating accounting records.		✓
The password will prevent theft of inventory and cash from the business.		✓

Explanation:

Technological products typically have a high retail price and are very popular making the risk of theft high. If a member of warehouse staff for example, had access to both the accounting records and the inventory in the warehouse, he/she could steal inventory and cover it up by altering the accounting records. Limiting access to the accounting records to the accounting department would prevent other members of staff covering up their theft.

The accounts department are likely to be made up of trainee and qualified accountants so best placed to maintain the accounting records.

However, the password would not prevent deliberate manipulation of accounting records by the accounts department as all members of the department have access to it. Nor will it prevent physical theft of inventory or cash – physical controls, such as needing a keycard to access the warehouse, would be appropriate here.

••

Task 2.10

	✓
A write down of a line of inventory at the year end from cost to NRV is it was sold at a loss in July 20X6	✓
A decrease in the allowance for doubtful debts because of a rise in the average number of days credit customers are taking to pay	
An increase in the useful life of plant and machinery to reduce the depreciation charge	
Posting a cash payment to the suspense account	

Explanation:

IAS 2 requires inventory to be valued at the lower of cost and net realisable value (NRV). Sale of goods at a loss post year end is an indication that NRV is lower than cost and therefore that the inventory must be written down. So this transaction appears genuine.

A rise in the average number of days credit customers are taking to pay would indication that the allowance for doubtful debts should be increased not decreased.

The useful life of plant and machinery should be increased if a business believes that it will be able to use the asset for longer than originally anticipated. Evidence of a useful life being too short would be a large profit on disposal. However, changing the useful life of an asset purely to reduce depreciation and increase profit is not acceptable.

The suspense account should only be used as a temporary account – for example, when an accountant is unsure where to post a double entry or to make a trial balance balance. However, it should never appear in the final accounts.

Task 2.11

	Appropriate ✓	Not appropriate ✓
Allowing the manager partner to review the year end accounts that you have prepared	✓	
Emailing the accounts to your friend who is thinking of applying for a job with the client		✓
Allowing the client's bank to access the accounts with the proprietor's permission	✓	
Allowing a credit supplier of your client access to the accounts when deciding whether or not to increase credit terms without authorisation from the proprietor		✓

Explanation:

Under the AAT's *Code of Professional Ethics*, following the fundamental principle of confidentiality means that client information should only be disclosed to third parties with permission from the client. The managing partner of your accounting practice does not qualify as a third party as your firm as a whole has been engaged to prepare the accounts of your client and in fact, the client would expect sign off from the managing partner.

●●●

Task 2.12

	Valid ✓	Not valid ✓
The accounting treatment is correct so there has been no breach of the AAT's *Code of Professional Ethics*.		✓
If this treatment was deliberate, there has been a breach of the fundamental principle of integrity.	✓	
If this treatment was a genuine error, there has been a breach of the fundamental principle of professional competence and due care.	✓	
There is a clear breach of confidentiality here requiring your firm to resign as accountants for this client.		✓

Explanation:

When an owner takes money out of the business, it is classified as drawings not an expense. Therefore, the client's accounting treatment is incorrect. As he is a trainee accounting technician, he is bound by the AAT's *Code of Professional Ethics*. If he knowingly and deliberately classified the drawings incorrectly as an expense, he appears to be trying to hide money that he is taking out of the business for personal use which would be a breach of the fundamental principle of integrity. However, if the treatment was a genuine error, there has been a breach of the fundamental principle of professional competence and due care as he has not followed the accounting treatment required by accounting standards.

There is no issue with confidentiality here. That would occur if we had disclosed client information to a third party without client consent.

Task 2.13

	✓
Self-interest	
Self-review	
Advocacy	
Familiarity	✓
Intimidation	

Explanation:

The client's close friendship with the managing partner introduces a familiarity threat because there is a risk of a breach of the fundamental principle of integrity when the managing partner reviews your work on the client's accounts. It is possible that the managing partner may put the client's personal interests before the business's best interests.

Task 2.14

£	155,300

Explanation:

Use the accounting equation to calculate capital.

Capital = Assets – Liabilities

Capital = £120,000 + £43,000 + £65,000 + £16,400 – £57,100 – £32,000

= £155,300

Task 2.15

£	294,800

Explanation:

The accounting equation is:

Capital = Assets – Liabilities

Closing capital = Opening capital + New capital introduced + Profit – Drawings

Closing capital = £250,000 + £12,000 + £37,500 – £4,700

= £294,800

Task 2.16

	✓
Capital – Liabilities = Assets	
Double entry bookkeeping is based on the accounting equation	✓
All elements of the accounting equation can be found in the statement of profit or loss	
Closing capital = Opening capital – Profit + Drawings	

Explanation:

The accounting equation is: Capital = Assets – Liabilities. This can also be stated as: Capital + Liabilities = Assets which makes the first option incorrect.

All elements of the accounting equation can be found in the statement of financial position but not the statement of profit or loss. This makes the third statement incorrect.

Closing capital = Opening capital + New capital introduced + Profit – Drawings. This makes the last option incorrect as the signs for profit and drawings are the wrong way round.

Double entry bookkeeping is based on the accounting equation as the fundamental concept of debits = credits is reflected with the equation Assets = Capital + Liabilities.

Task 2.17

	Increase ✓	Decrease ✓	No change ✓
Assets	✓		
Liabilities			✓
Capital	✓		

Task 2.18

	✓
To ensure that you understand your responsibilities	
To ensure that the company meets all of its legal responsibilities	✓
To make it easy for you to complete your day-to-day tasks	
To improve your technical knowledge	

Task 2.19

	✓
You have been asked to account for a provision but you are unsure how to do this, so you make a guess at the appropriate treatment.	
A client has given you tickets to a high profile football match. The next day they ask you to ignore the liquidation of a customer that owes the client a substantial amount of money.	
Your firm needs to meet its deadline in preparing the accounts. Your supervisor tells you to save time by just repeating the depreciation entry from last year, rather than recalculating it.	
The bank statement for your firm shows that an insurance bill covering the next accounting period has been paid in the current accounting period. Your manager asks you to make a prepayment for the cost of the insurance.	✓

Chapter 3

Task 3.1

Expenditure	Capital expenditure £	Revenue expenditure £
A machine has been purchased at a cost of £12,000. The delivery charge was £400.	12,400	0
A building has been purchased at a cost of £120,000. The building is subsequently re-decorated at a cost of £13,000.	120,000	13,000
A new main server has been purchased at a cost of £10,000. Professional fees of £200 were also incurred, as a result of this expenditure.	10,200	0

Explanation:

Expenditure on the machine exceeds the threshold for capitalisation. The cost of the machine (£12,000) and the associated delivery charges (£400) meet the definition of non-current asset expenditure and are therefore capitalised as a non-current asset.

Expenditure on the building is also capital in nature and exceeds the threshold for capitalisation. Again, it is classified as capital expenditure. However, costs of redecorating the building constitute revenue expenditure. Therefore, the £13,000 is excluded from the cost of the non-current asset and instead expensed to the profit or loss account.

Expenditure on the main server (£10,000) is capital expenditure. The professional fees of £200 are also capitalised as part of the cost of the asset. At £200, in themselves they are below the capitalisation threshold for this business. However, they contribute to the cost of the main server which exceeds the level at which assets are capitalised and therefore are recorded as a non-current asset.

Task 3.2

£	48,000

Explanation:

The non-current asset is capitalised at the VAT-inclusive amount of £48,000. The business is not VAT registered and is therefore is unable to reclaim the VAT on this purchase from the tax authorities. Consequently, the VAT is added to the cost of the asset.

Task 3.3

Description	Method
The vending machines in a business's premises were financed by paying an initial deposit to the finance company followed by a fixed number of instalments. After all instalments have been paid, the vending machines will be owned by the business.	Hire purchase
When a business purchases a new motor vehicle, the old vehicle is given to the dealer to cover part of the cost of the new vehicle.	Part-exchange
Factory equipment is acquired as part of a major refurbishment. The bank provides the funding, which is then paid back in instalments over an agreed period of time, together with interest.	Loan

Task 3.4

Details	Acquisition date	Cost £	Funding method
HF405	01/06/X4	13,550.00	Finance lease

Explanation:

Item HF405 is capitalised at a cost of £13,550.00. It was acquired on 01/06/X4 and funded through a finance lease. The boardroom table, table fittings and delivery costs are all part of this non-current asset and therefore included as part of the total cost.

In particular, although the delivery costs (£450) are below the level of capitalisation (£500), they contribute to the part of the cost of the boardroom table which is greater than the capitalisation threshold. Therefore, the delivery costs are capitalised as part of the cost of this non-current asset.

The chairs (details PN2948) are below the level for capitalisation and therefore are not recorded in the solution above. For this reason, no entries are made in the second row of the data entry table.

Task 3.5

Account	Debit £	Credit £
Machine at cost	19,200	
Bank		19,200

Working:

VAT: £16,000 × 20% = £3,200

Cost of the machine: £16,000 plus £3,200 = £19,200

As the business is not registered for VAT, the VAT cannot be reclaimed from the tax authorities. Therefore, it is added to the cost of the asset.

Task 3.6

Machine at cost

	£		£
Balance b/d	24,500	**Balance c/d**	**38,000**
Bank	**13,500**		
	38,000		**38,000**

Bank

	£		£	
Balance b/d	32,000	**Machine at cost**	**13,500**	⎤ Gross:
		VAT control account	**2,700**	⎬ 16,200
		Balance c/d	**15,800**	⎦
	32,000		**32,000**	

VAT control account

	£		£
Bank	**2,700**	Balance b/d	5,000
Balance c/d	**2,300**		
	5,000		**5,000**

Explanation:

This business is registered for VAT and therefore can generally reclaim VAT on purchases from the tax authorities. For this reason, the VAT levied on the asset it is not capitalised as part of its cost. Instead it is debited to the VAT control account. The VAT on the new machine is calculated as: £13,500 × 20% = £2,700. The amount paid from Bank is the amount gross of VAT: £13,500 + £2,700 = £16,200 (alternatively calculated as £13,500 × 1.2 = £16,200).

··

Task 3.7

	✓
On non-current assets, including repairs and maintenance	
On expensive assets	
Relating to the acquisition or improvement of non-current assets	✓

Explanation:

Expenditure relating to the acquisition or improvement of non-current assets constitutes capital expenditure. Repairs and maintenance expenditure qualifies as revenue rather than capital expenditure.

Whilst non-current assets may be expensive, 'expensive assets' is not a criteria for capitalisation.

··

Task 3.8

Description	Term
Expenditure for the trade of the business or to repair, maintain and service non-current assets.	Revenue expenditure
Expenditure for the acquisition, replacement or improvement of non-current assets.	Capital expenditure

Explanation:

It is important to distinguish between capital and revenue expenditure.

Capital expenditure results in a non-current asset in the statement of financial position. Revenue expenditure results in an expense in the statement of profit or loss and therefore a reduction in profit.

Task 3.9

Description	Impact	Amount £
Statement of financial position	**Increase non-current assets**	**517,300**
Statement of profit or loss	**Reduce profit**	**8,700**

Explanation:

When a business buys a non-current asset, the purchase price plus directly attributable costs are capitalised. At £500,000, the property is well in excess of the capitalisation threshold. The amount to be capitalised as a non-current asset in the statement of financial position is £517,300 (£500,000 + £15,000 + £2,300).

The repairs are revenue rather than capital expenditure and therefore, the £8,700 should be recorded as an expense in the statement of profit or loss. This will have the effect of reducing profit.

Task 3.10

It is important to obtain prior authority for capital expenditure in order to ensure that: the assets are necessary to the business and purchased at the best price.

The business's solicitor would not be the most appropriate person to give this authority.

Explanation:

Authorising capital expenditure does not ensure that the assets are correctly recorded in either the non-current assets register or the general ledger. An accounts department supervisor reviewing the bookkeeper's entries would, for example, be in a better position to check that non-current asset purchases are recorded accurately.

The purpose of authorisation is to ensure that the business as a whole will benefit from the purchase.

A person internal to the business rather than the external solicitor would be the most appropriate person to authorise the expenditure. For a small business, the owner might wish to authorise all capital expenditure. For a larger business, a department supervisor or manager might be more appropriate.

Task 3.11

	✓
Bank loan	✓
Cash purchase	
Finance lease	
Hire purchase	

Explanation:

A cash purchase would not be appropriate here because the business only has a cash balance of £750 yet the asset costs well in excess of that amount at £100,000. As the business wishes to become legal owner with immediate effect, neither a finance lease or hire purchase agreement would be appropriate. Therefore, a bank loan would be the best option here.

Task 3.12

Account	Amount £	Debit ✓	Credit ✓
Bank	10,000	✓	
Loan	10,000		✓

Account	Amount £	Debit ✓	Credit ✓
Motor vehicles at cost	9,800	✓	
Bank	9,800		✓

Explanation:

The receipt of the loan results in an increase in the bank account. Bank is an asset and therefore a debit is required. The corresponding credit is to the loan account which is a liability as the business now owes money to the bank.

Then the actual purchase of the asset is recorded by debiting the motor vehicles at cost account, being an increase in non-current assets. The corresponding credit entry is to bank, as this asset is now decreasing.

Chapter 4

Task 4.1

	✓
To spread the cost of a non-current asset over its useful life in order to match the cost of the asset with the consumption of the asset's economic benefits	✓
To ensure that funds are available for the eventual replacement of the asset	
To reduce the cost of the asset to its estimated market value	
To recognise the fact that assets lose their value over time	

Task 4.2

Depreciation is an application of the accruals basis of accounting.

Task 4.3

(a)

Depreciation charge £	Carrying amount £
3,480	6,960

Working:

Depreciation charge: £17,400/5 years = £3,480

Carrying amount: £17,400 – (3 × £3,480) = £6,960

(b)

Depreciation charge £	Carrying amount £
2,700	7,400

Working:

Depreciation charge:

$$\frac{12,800-2,000}{4 \text{ years}} = £2,700$$

Carrying amount: £12,800 – (2 × £2,700) = £7,400

(c)

Depreciation charge £	Carrying amount £
1,300	3,300

Working:

Depreciation charge:

$$\frac{4,600-700}{3 \text{ years}} = £1,300$$

Carrying amount: £4,600 – £1,300 = £3,300

....

Task 4.4

(a)

Depreciation charge £	Carrying amount £
4,920	19,680

Workings:

Depreciation charge for the year end 31 March 20X9: £24,600 × 20% = £4,920

Carrying amount as at 31 March 20X9: £24,600 – £4,920 = £19,680

(b)

Depreciation charge £	Carrying amount £
608	2,432

Workings:

Depreciation charge for the year end 31 March 20X8: £3,800 × 20% = £760 (even though the motor vehicle was only owned for 5 months of the year, the accounting policy is to charge a full year's depreciation in the year of acquisition and so no pro-rating is required)

Carrying amount as at 31 March 20X8: £3,800 – £760 = £3,040

Depreciation charge for the year end 31 March 20X9: £3,040 × 20% = £608

Carrying amount as at 31 March 20X9: £3,040 – £608 = £2,432

Task 4.5

(a)

Depreciation charge £	Accumulated depreciation £
7,200	7,200

Working:

Depreciation charge for the year end 31 March 20X9: £24,000 × 30% = £7,200

Accumulated depreciation at 31 March 20X9 = £7,200 (as the business has only owned the asset for one year)

(b)

Depreciation charge £	Accumulated depreciation £
3,927	9,537

Working:

Depreciation charge for the year end 31 March 20X8: £18,700 × 30% = £5,610 (even though the asset was only owned for 8 months in the year, no pro-rating is required as the accounting policy is to charge a full year in the year of acquisition)

Accumulated depreciation at 31 March 20X8 = £5,610

Depreciation charge for the year end 31 March 20X9: (£18,700 – £5,610) × 30% = £3,927

Accumulated depreciation at 31 March 20X9: £5,610 + £3,927 = £9,537

Task 4.6

(a)

Depreciation charge £	Carrying amount £
2,000	13,000

Working:

Depreciation charge for the year end 31 December 20X8: £15,000 × 20% × 8/12 = £2,000

Carrying amount for the year end 31 December 20X8: £15,000 – £2,000 = £13,000

(b)

Depreciation charge £	Carrying amount £
280	3,920

Working:

Depreciation charge for the year end 31 December 20X8: £4,200 × 40% × 2/12 = £280

Carrying amount for the year end 31 December 20X8: £4,200 – £280 = £3,920

Task 4.7

Year	Number of units produced	Carrying amount b/d £	Depreciation charges £	Accumulated depreciation £	Carrying amount c/d £
1	90,000	120,000	36,000	36,000	84,000
2	72,000	84,000	28,800	64,800	55,200
3	30,000	55,200	12,000	76,800	43,200

Workings:

Year	Working	Depreciation charge
1	90,000 / 300,000 × 120,000	36,000
2	72,000 / 300,000 × 120,000	28,800
3	30,000 / 300,000 × 120,000	12,000

Task 4.8

	Account
Debit	Depreciation charges
Credit	Vehicles accumulated depreciation

Explanation:

This is the journal to record depreciation in the general ledger. Depreciation charges are a debit entry being an increase in expenses. Vehicles accumulated depreciation is a credit entry being a reduction in the carrying amount of the asset.

Task 4.9

Vehicles at cost

	£		£
Balance b/d	50,600	**Balance c/d**	**58,800**
Bank	**8,200**		
	58,800		**58,800**

Depreciation charges

	£		£
Balance b/d	12,300	**Profit or loss account**	**13,850**
Vehicles accumulated depreciation	**1,550**		
	13,850		**13,850**

Vehicles accumulated depreciation

	£		£
Balance c/d	**25,950**	Balance b/d	24,400
		Depreciation charges	**1,550**
	25,950		**25,950**

Working:

Depreciation on new vehicle = (Cost £8,200 less residual value £2,000) / 4 = £1,550 (even though the asset was only owned for 9 months in the year, no pro-rating is required as the accounting policy is that a full year's depreciation is applied in the year of acquisition)

■■

Task 4.10

(a)

Depreciation method	✓
Diminishing balance method	
Straight line method	
Units of production method	✓

(b)

Depreciation method	✓
Diminishing balance method	
Straight line method	✓
Units of production method	

(c)

Depreciation method	✓
Diminishing balance method	✓
Straight line method	
Units of production method	

Task 4.11

Percentage: [2] %

Apply to: [Cost]

Explanation:

The percentage is calculated as: $1/50 \times 100\% = 2\%$

As the straight line method is used, it is applied to the cost of the asset rather than the carrying amount.

Chapter 5

Task 5.1

		Gain	Loss
£	125		✓

Workings:

Gain or loss on disposal working	£
Proceeds	6,000
Less carrying amount at date of disposal*	(6,125)
Loss on disposal	(125)
Carrying amount at date of disposal:	
Cost	12,500
Less depreciation for year ended 31 March 20X7 (£12,500 × 30%)	(3,750)
Carrying amount at end of year 1	8,750
Less depreciation for year ended 31 March 20X8 (£8,750 × 30%)	(2,625)
Carrying amount at date of disposal	6,125*

Explanation:

Even though the machine was sold six months into the current year end of 31 March 20X9, there is no depreciation charge for the year as the business's policy is to charge a full year's depreciation in the year of acquisition and none in the year of disposal.

Task 5.2

		Gain	Loss
£	132	✓	

Workings:

Gain or loss on disposal working	£
Proceeds	5,100
Less carrying amount at date of disposal *	(4,968)
Gain on disposal	132
Carrying amount at date of disposal:	
Cost	13,800
Less depreciation for year ended 31 March 20X5 (£13,800 × 40%)	(5,520)
Carrying amount at end of year 1	8,280
Less depreciation for year ended 31 March 20X6 (£8,280 × 40%)	(3,312)
Carrying amount at date of disposal	4,968*

Explanation:

Even though the machine was sold three months into the current year end of 31 March 20X7, there is no depreciation charge for the year as the business's policy is to charge a full year's depreciation in the year of acquisition and none in the year of disposal.

Task 5.3

	Answer
The gain or loss arising on disposal of a non-current asset is recorded in the	statement of profit or loss
In the business's accounts, the carrying amount of non-current assets is entered in the	statement of financial position
The carrying amount of a non-current asset is calculated as the cost of the asset less the	accumulated depreciation

Task 5.4

(a)

£	10,000

Working:

Annual depreciation charge: (25,000 /5) = £5,000

Accumulated depreciation at 31 December 20X4 = £5,000 for year ended 31 December 20X3 + £5,000 for the year ended 31 December 20X4 = £10,000.

No depreciation is charged in the year ended 31 December 20X5, the year of disposal.

(b)

Machine at cost

	£		£
Balance b/d	60,000	**Disposals**	**25,000**
		Balance c/d	**35,000**
	60,000		**60,000**

Bank

	£		£
Balance b/d	22,000	**Balance c/d**	**34,000**
Disposals	**12,000**		
	34,000		**34,000**

Machine accumulated depreciation

	£		£
Disposals	**10,000**	Balance b/d	26,000
Balance c/d	**16,000**		
	26,000		**26,000**

Disposals

	£		£
Machine at cost	**25,000**	**Machine accumulated depreciation**	**10,000**
		Bank	**12,000**
		Profit or loss account	**3,000**
	25,000		**25,000**

(c)

The business has made a **loss** on disposal of the machine.

Explanation:

The carrying amount of £15,000 (cost £25,000 less accumulated depreciation £10,000) exceeds the sale proceeds of £12,000. Therefore, a loss on disposal of £3,000 arises.

The loss is credited to the disposals account. In the general ledger, the corresponding debit is to the profit or loss account, being an increase in expenses and therefore a reduction in profit for the year.

Task 5.5

(a)

Account	Amount £	Debit ✓	Credit ✓
Bank	4,500	✓	
Disposals	4,500		✓

(b)

Account	Amount £	Debit	Credit
Disposals	20,000	✓	
Office equipment at cost	20,000		✓

Explanation:

When a non-current asset is disposed of, all financial transactions relating to that asset will be transferred to the disposals account.

Where bank proceeds are received on sale of a non-current asset, there is a debit to the bank general ledger account, being an increase in the bank asset and a corresponding credit the disposals account.

Removing the original cost of the equipment from the general ledger requires a credit to the office equipment at cost account, being a decrease in the asset and a corresponding debit to the disposals account.

· ·

Task 5.6

Disposal account

	£		£
Machine at cost	15,600	Machine accumulated depreciation	9,425
		Bank	6,000
		Profit or loss account	175
	15,600		15,600

Explanation:

On disposal the machine must be removed from the general ledger. Therefore, the cost of the machine and the machine accumulated depreciation are transferred to the disposals account.

Having included the sales proceeds in the disposals account, the disposals account can be totalled. The balancing figure is the gain or loss arising on disposal of the asset.

In this scenario, a loss has arisen on disposal of the non-current asset as the carrying amount at the date of disposal (machine at cost £15,600 less machine accumulated depreciation £9,425 = carrying amount £6,175) is less than the sales proceeds (£6,000).

Workings:

Accumulated depreciation at the date of disposal:

Depreciation period	Calculation	£
01.07.X6 to 31.12.X6	$15,600 \times 25\% \times 6/12$	1,950
01.01.X7 to 31.12.X7	$15,600 \times 25\%$	3,900
01.01.X8 to 30.11.X8	$15,600 \times 25\% \times 11/12$	3,575
		9,425

Task 5.7

	✓
To record non-current assets in the general ledger	
To assist in the physical verification of non-current assets and check the accuracy of the general ledger entries relating to tangible non-current assets	✓
To list all intangible non-current assets of the business	
To authorise capital expenditure	

Explanation:

The non-current assets register is a list of all the tangible non-current assets owned by the business. It is part of the business's internal control system rather than its double entry system.

It helps with the physical verification of the assets as it can be checked that tangible assets are recorded in the register and that the assets in the register actually exist. Also, the accuracy of the non-current asset general ledger entries can be checked by reconciling the general ledger entries with the non-current asset register.

The non-current asset register does not include intangible non-current assets. The authorisation of capital expenditure is typically shown on authorisation forms rather than in the non-current assets register.

Task 5.8

Extract from non-current assets register

Description	Acquisition date	Cost £	Depreciation charges £	Carrying amount £	Funding method	Disposal proceeds £	Disposal date
Plant and machinery							
Plant PM672	01/04/X6	3,300.00			Cash		
Year end 30/06/X6			165.00	3,135.00			

Explanation:

The purchase price of plant PM672 of £3,000.00 plus any directly attributable costs which include the testing costs of £300.00 must be capitalised. Even though the testing costs are below the capitalisation threshold of £400.00, they relate to an asset which has met the capitalisation threshold (with its purchase price of £3,000.00). Therefore, they must also be capitalised as part of the cost. This means the item is capitalised at a total cost of £3,300.00.

The maintenance contract qualifies as revenue expenditure and therefore the £550.00 is not capitalised. As the business is VAT registered, it may reclaim VAT on purchases so the VAT should not be included in the cost of the asset.

Depreciation = £3,300.00 × 1/5 × 3/12 = £165.00.

Task 5.9

Extract from non-current assets register

Description	Acquisition date	Cost £	Depreciation charges £	Carrying amount £	Funding method	Disposal proceeds £	Disposal date
Office equipment							
Desk DSK452	01/06/X5	2,500.00			Loan		
Year end 31/12/X5			625.00	1,875.00			
Year end 31/12/X6			468.75	1,406.25			
Year end 31/12/X7			0.00	0.00		800.00	30/09/X7

Explanation:

The policy here is no depreciation in the year of disposal. On disposal, the carrying amount is zero as the item is effectively removed both from both the business and the accounting records.

The disposal proceeds and disposal date must be recorded in the non-current assets register.

Task 5.10

Extract from the non-current assets register

Description	Acquisition date	Cost £	Depreciation charges £	Carrying amount £	Funding method	Disposal proceeds £	Disposal date
Office equipment							
Computer COM987	01/04/X1	5,700.00			Part exchange		
Year end 31/03/X2			1,140.00	4,560.00			
Year end 31/03/X3			1,140.00	3,420.00			
Year end 31/12/X4			855.00	0.00		1,300.00	01/01/X4

Explanation:

As the policy is to charge depreciation on a monthly pro-rata basis, depreciation in the year ended 31 March 20X4 is: £5,700.00 × 20% × 9/12 = £855.00. As the asset has been sold, the carrying amount is now zero. Finally, the proceeds and disposal date must also be recorded.

....

Task 5.11

Description/ Serial number	Acquisition date	Cost £	Depreciation charges £	Carrying amount £	Funding method	Disposal proceeds £	Disposal date
Furniture and fittings							
Filing racks	31/10/X5	832.60			Cash		
Year end 31/03/X6			124.89	707.71			
Year end 31/03/X7			**124.89**	**582.82**			
Oak boardroom table	**24/06/X6**	**925.00**			**Loan**		
Year end 31/03/X7			**138.75**	**786.25**			
Motor vehicles							
1.6 litre car AF05 LKR	01/09/X4	10,600.00			Part-exchange		
Year end 31/03/X5			2,650.00	7,950.00			
Year end 31/03/X6			1,987.50	5,962.50			
Year end 31/03/X7			**0.00**	**0.00**		**5,340.00**	**23/09/X6**
1.8 litre van AD05 ACT	01/03/X5	10,400.00			Part-exchange		
Year end 31/03/X5			2,600.00	7,800.00			
Year end 31/03/X6			1,950.00	5,850.00			
Year end 31/03/X7			**1,462.50**	**4,387.50**			

BPP
LEARNING MEDIA

Explanation:

Depreciation for filing racks = £832.60 × 15% = £124.89

Oak boardroom table: Capitalise purchase price £850.00 + Direct costs £75.00 = £925.00. Depreciation = £925.00 × 15% = £138.75 (a full year's depreciation is charged in the year of acquisition). The maintenance and repair kit is revenue expenditure and therefore is not capitalised.

Each refurbished operator chair at £60 each is below the £350 capitalisation threshold and so these chairs are not capitalised.

1.6 litre car AF05 LKR: No depreciation is charged in the year of disposal and on disposal, the carrying amount is reduced to £0.00. The sales proceeds and disposal date are then recorded.

1.8 litre van AD05 ACT: Depreciation = £5,850.00 × 25% = £1,462.50.

Task 5.12

Description/ Serial number	Acquisition date	Cost £	Depreciation charges £	Carrying amount £	Funding method	Disposal Proceeds £	Disposal date
Office equipment							
Copier 4	01/04/X5	3,200.00			Finance lease		
Year end 31/03/X6			400.00	2,800.00			
Year end 31/03/X7			**400.00**	**2,400.00**			
Reception desk – FaradyR	01/01/X5	1,200.00			Cash		
Year end 31/03/X5			37.50	1,162.50			
Year end 31/03/X6			150.00	1,012.50			
Year end 31/03/X7			**75.00**	**0.00**		600.00	30/09/X6

Description/ Serial number	Acquisition date	Cost £	Depreciation charges £	Carrying amount £	Funding method	Disposal Proceeds £	Disposal date
Machinery							
CNC machine CNC3491	01/04/X4	16,400.00			Part-exchange		
Year end 31/03/X5			4,100.00	12,300.00			
Year end 31/03/X6			3,075.00	9,225.00			
Year end 31/03/X7			**2,306.25**	**6,918.75**			
Power lathe PM892	**01/04/X6**	**10,189.80**			**Hire purchase**		
Year end 31/03/X7			**2,547.45**	**7,642.35**			

Explanation:

Copier 4: Depreciation = £3,200 × 1/8 = £400.00

Reception desk – FaradyR: Depreciation = £1,200 × 1/8 × 6/12 = £75.00 (as depreciation is charged on a monthly pro-rata basis). On disposal, the carrying amount is reduced to £0.00 and the disposal proceeds and date are recorded.

CNC machine CNC3491: Depreciation = £9,225.00 × 25% = £2,306.25

Power lather PM892: The purchase price of £9,930.00 + direct costs £259.80 = £10,189.80 are capitalised. The maintenance contract is revenue expenditure so is not capitalised. QW Trading is VAT registered and therefore can recover the VAT on this purchase from HMRC. For this reason, VAT is not included as part of the cost of the asset.

Depreciation = £10,189.80 × 25% = £2,547.45.

....

Task 5.13

(a)

(i)

£	1,350

Working:

	£
1 January 20X3: Cost	3,500
Depreciation (15% × 3,500)	(525)
31 July 20X3	2,975
Depreciation (15% × 2,975)	(446)
31 July 20X4	2,529
Depreciation (15% × 2,529)	(379)
31 July 20X5	2,150

Accumulated depreciation at disposal = £525 + £446 + £379 = £1,350

(ii) Disposals

	£		£
Machinery at cost	3,500	**Machinery accumulated depreciation**	1,350
		Machinery at cost	575
		Profit or loss account	1,575
	3,500		**3,500**

(b)

(i)

£	2,725.00

Working

Cost of new machinery = Part exchange value £575 + cash paid £2,150 = £2,725

(ii) The machinery at cost account will have a final balance carried down

of £ | 25,045 | when the ledger accounts are closed

for the year.

Working

Machines at cost

	£		£
Balance b/d	25,820	Disposals	3,500
Disposals	575		
Bank	2,150	Balance c/d	25,045
	28,545		28,545

Chapter 6

Task 6.1

(a) Telephone expenses

	£		£
Bank	845	Profit or loss account	1,015
Accrued expenses	170		
	1,015		1,015

(b)

The reversal of this accrual is dated ⟨ 1 April 20X6 ⟩ .

The reversal is on the ⟨ credit ⟩ side of the telephone expenses account.

Task 6.2

Electricity expense

	£		£
Bank	**2,300**	**Accrued expenses (reversal)**	**370**
Accrued expenses (2/3 × £900)	**600**	**Profit or loss account**	**2,530**
	2,900		**2,900**

Accrued expenses (SOFP)

	£		£
Electricity expense	**370**	Balance b/d	370
Balance c/d	**600**	**Electricity expense**	**600**
	970		**970**

Task 6.3

Insurance expense

	£		£
Prepaid expenses (reversal)	180	Prepaid expenses	250
Bank	2,300	Profit or loss account	2,230
	2,480		2,480

Task 6.4

Prepaid expenses

	£		£
Balance b/d	300	**Rent expense**	300
Rent expense (3/6 × £800)	400	**Balance c/d**	400
	700		700

Task 6.5

(a)

£	5,610

Explanation:

This is calculated as the cash book receipts of £5,600 less the £490 received in relation to the prior year plus the amount outstanding for June 20X3 at the year end (1/3 × £1,500 = £500). This comes to £5,610 (£5,600 – £490 + £500).

Alternatively, you could have drawn up the ledger account for rental income:

Rental income

	£		£
Accrued income (reversal)	490	Bank	5,600
Profit or loss account	5,610	Accrued income (1/3 × £1,500)	500
	6,100		6,100

(b)

Reason for considering the receipt dated 10 September 20X3	Acceptable reason	Not acceptable reason
The accruals concept requires income to be recorded in the financial statements in the period in which it is earned.	✓	
The proprietor of the business has asked you to increase the profit for the year to maximise his chances of increasing the business' overdraft limit.		✓
The transaction results in a current liability for June's rental income as at 30 June 20X3.		✓

Explanation:

Under the AAT's *Code of Professional Ethics*, as an accountant, we are required to act with Professional Competence and Care which means that when preparing accounts, we should follow International Financial Reporting Standards and concepts. This makes the first option acceptable. However, we should not act purely on the motivation of self-interest of the proprietor which makes the second option not acceptable. Finally, the transaction results in a current asset not a current liability at 30 June 20X3, making the final option not acceptable.

Task 6.6

	✓
Overstated by £375	
Overstated by £750	
Understated by £375	
Understated by £750	✓

Explanation:

An accrual of £375 should have been set up, which would have increased the electricity expense for the year by £375 and resulted in accrued expenses of £375 (a current liability). Instead a prepayment was set up, decreasing the expense by £375 and resulting in prepaid expenses of £375 (a current asset). Setting up the prepayment instead of an accrual has therefore understated the expense for the year by £750 (2 × £375). The correcting journal would be:

Debit Electricity expense	£750
Credit Prepaid expenses	£375
Credit Accrued expenses	£375

Task 6.7

£	20,388.23

Working:

	£
Paid in year (£7,279.47 + £4,663.80 + £4,117.28)	16,060.55
Accrual (2/3 × £6,491.52)	4,327.68
	20,388.23

Task 6.8

£	900

Working:

Rent expense

	£		£
Bank	1,275	Accrued expenses (reversal)	250
		Prepaid expenses (1/3 × £375)	125
		Profit or loss account	900
	1,275		1,275

Task 6.9

	✓
£4,000	
£4,500	✓
£5,000	
£5,500	

Working:

Commission income

	£		£
Accrued income (reversal)	1,000	Bank	5,000
Profit or loss account	4,500	Accrued income	500
	5,500		5,500

Task 6.10

(a)

	Amount £	Debit	Credit
Prepaid income	850	✓	
Maintenance services income	850		✓

(b) Maintenance services income

	£		£
Prepaid income (6/12 × £3,000)	1,500	Prepaid income (reversal)	850
Profit or loss account	12,100	Bank	12,750
	13,600		13,600

Task 6.11

(a) Service income

	£		£
Accrued income (reversal)	210	**Bank**	**1,680**
Profit or loss account	**1,655**	**Accrued income**	**185**
	1,865		**1,865**

(b)

(i)

	Increase ✓	Decrease ✓	No change ✓
Assets		✓	
Liabilities			✓
Equity		✓	

Explanation:

The accounting entry to reverse the accrued income is:

| DEBIT (↓) Service income (SPL) | £210 | |
| CREDIT (↓) Accrued income (SOFP) | | £210 |

The debit to service income decreases the profit for the year and therefore also decreases retained earnings and equity.

Accrued income is an asset account (amounts owed to the business) and therefore a debit balance in the trial balance.

Therefore, a credit to accrued income results in a decrease in assets.

The above double entry has no impact on liabilities.

(ii)

	✓
1 April 20X5	✓
31 March 20X5	
31 March 20X6	

(c)

Prepaid expenses	of	£15	dated	**31 March 20X6**

(d)

£	577

Working:

Insurance

	£		£
		Accrued insurance (reversal)	78
		Prepaid expenses	**15**
Bank	670	**Profit or loss account**	**577**
	670		**670**

Chapter 7

Task 7.1

(a)

£	25.10

Working: £24.60 + £0.50

(b)

£	24.80

Working: £25.80 – £1.00

(c)

£	3,100

Working: 125 units × £24.80

Explanation:

Inventory is recorded at the lower of cost and net realisable value, hence being valued at £24.80 unit in this scenario.

....

Task 7.2

	✓
Selling costs	
Cost of purchase, including delivery	✓
Storage costs of finished goods	
Costs of conversion, including direct labour	✓

Explanation:

Under IAS 2 *Inventories*, selling costs and storage costs of finished goods cannot be included in the cost of inventory.

....

Task 7.3

	✓
The expected selling price of the inventory	
The expected selling price of the inventory less costs to completion and selling costs	✓
The replacement cost of the inventory	
The market price of the inventory	

Explanation:

Net realisable value is the amount that can be obtained, less any further future expenses to be incurred to bring the inventory to a condition in which it can be sold.

....

Task 7.4

The rule for inventory is that it should be valued at the | **lower** |

of | **cost** | and | **net realisable value** |

....

Task 7.5

(a) and (b)

Inventory line	Quantity (units)	Cost £	Selling price £	Selling costs £	Net realisable value £	Value per unit £	Total value £
A	180	12.50	20.40	0.50	19.90	12.50	2,250
B	240	10.90	12.60	1.80	10.80	10.80	2,592
C	300	15.40	22.70	1.20	21.50	15.40	4,620
D	80	16.50	17.80	1.50	16.30	16.30	1,304
E	130	10.60	18.00	1.00	17.00	10.60	1,378
Total							12,144

Explanation:

Inventory is valued at the lower of cost and net realisable value on a line by line basis. Therefore, inventory lines A, C and E are valued at cost. Inventory lines B and D are valued at net realisable value.

....

Task 7.6

(a)

Description	Method of estimating cost
Under this method a simple average cost can be calculated whereby the cost of all purchases/production during the year is divided by the total number of units purchased.	Average cost
Under this method it is assumed that the last goods to be purchased/produced will be the first to be sold.	Last in first out
Under this method it is assumed that the first goods purchased/produced will be the first to be sold.	First in first out

(b)

Question	Answer
Is LIFO permitted by International Financial Reporting Standards?	No

Explanation:

The Last in first out (LIFO) method is prohibited by international International Financial Reporting Standards because it is unlikely to produce a cost figure which is a close approximation to actual costs.

....

Task 7.7

Account	Debit £	Credit £
Closing inventory (SOFP)	20,000	
Closing inventory (SPL)		20,000

Explanation:

Inventory is an asset in the statement of financial position, and therefore a debit balance in the general ledger.

Inventory is a reduction in expenses in the statement of profit or loss, and therefore a credit entry in the general ledger.

Task 7.8

Statement	Term
Closing inventory in the statement of financial position is best described as	an asset
Closing inventory in the statement of profit or loss is best described as	a reduction in expenses

Explanation:

Closing inventory is owned by the business at the year end. It can be sold in the next accounting period and will generate economic benefits for the business. Therefore, it is an asset in the statement of financial position.

In the statement or profit or loss closing inventory is included under the 'cost of goods sold' heading. It is a reduction in the cost of goods sold expense, as the items have not been sold in the current accounting period.

Task 7.9

Statement	True or false
In the statement of profit or loss, carriage inwards must be included within cost of goods sold.	True
In the statement of profit or loss, carriage outwards must be included within cost of goods sold.	False

Explanation:

Statement 1: Carriage inwards (ie the cost of transporting inventory to the businesses premises) forms part of cost of goods sold, along with opening inventory and purchases.

Statement 2: Carriage outwards (ie the cost of transporting inventory to customers) is part of selling expenses which sit below the gross profit line.

Task 7.10

Statement	True or false
The main purpose of an inventory count is to value inventory at the end of the accounting period.	False
On a regular basis an inventory reconciliation should be performed, comparing the warehouse's record of the quantity of each item held with the actual quantity counted.	True

Explanation:

Statement 1: The main purpose of an inventory count is to ascertain the quantity of inventory on hand at the end of the accounting period.

Statement 2: An inventory reconciliation must be performed on a regular basis, so that the business can confirm that its inventory records are accurate.

Task 7.11

Accounting for inventory as a deduction from cost of goods sold in the statement profit or loss is an application of the ⟨accruals⟩ basis of accounting.

Explanation:

In cost of goods sold, we only want to show the purchase price of goods actually sold in the period to match to the sales price of goods sold which is included in revenue. This is why we remove from purchases any goods that have not been sold in the year with the closing inventory adjustment in the statement of profit or loss at the year end.

Task 7.12

£	6,000

Working:

Selling price (net of VAT) = £12,000 × 100/120 = £10,000
Cost = Selling price £10,000 – Profit £4,000 = £6,000

As the business is VAT-registered, it must charge VAT on its sales and then pass this VAT onto HMRC.

However, when calculating the cost of the inventory, VAT is excluded from the selling price because it does not belong to the business. Then, to calculate the cost of the inventory, the profit is deducted from the net selling price.

Chapter 8

Task 8.1

Account	Debit £	Credit £
Irrecoverable debts	4,500	
Sales ledger control account		4,500

Explanation:

If a debt is irrecoverable it must be removed from the sales ledger control account as it is no longer an asset. It is written off as an expense in the irrecoverable debts account.

••

Task 8.2

(a)

Account	Debit £	Credit £
Irrecoverable debts	6,900	
Sales ledger control account		6,900

(b)

Sales ledger control account

	£		£
Balance b/d	45,000	**Irrecoverable debts**	**6,900**
		Balance c/d	**38,100**
	45,000		**45,000**

Irrecoverable debts

	£		£
Sales ledger control account	**6,900**	**Profit or loss account**	**6,900**
	6,900		**6,900**

(c)

ZX – Sales ledger account

	£		£
Balance b/d	6,900	**Irrecoverable debts**	**6,900**
	6,900		**6,900**

Task 8.3

Account	Debit £	Credit £
Bank	9,500	
Irrecoverable debts		9,500

Explanation:

As the debt has already been written off, it is no longer listed in the sales ledger and so the cash received cannot be offset against it in the usual way. Therefore, the cash received is offset against the irrecoverable debt expense in the current accounting period. In other words, it is a reduction in the current period irrecoverable debt expense.

Task 8.4

(a)

£	1,720

Working:

Trade receivables £86,000 × 2% = £1,720

(b)

£	560	Increase in expenses

Working:

	£
Opening allowance (per scenario)	1,160
Adjustment	560
Closing allowance	1,720

Explanation:

The closing allowance of £1,720 is higher than the opening allowance of £1,160. Therefore, expenses are increased as a result of the allowance for doubtful debts adjustment.

···

Task 8.5

Sales ledger control account

	£		£
Balance b/d	90,000	**Irrecoverable debts**	**4,400**
		Balance c/d	**85,600**
	90,000		**90,000**

Irrecoverable debts

	£		£
Sales ledger control account	**4,400**	**Profit or loss account**	**4,400**
	4,400		**4,400**

Allowance for doubtful debts

	£		£
Balance c/d	**4,672**	Balance b/d	1,600
		Allowance for doubtful debts – adjustments	**3,072**
	4,672		**4,672**

Allowance for doubtful debts – adjustments

	£		£
Allowance for doubtful debts	3,072	Profit or loss account	3,072
	3,072		3,072

Working:

	£
Opening balance per sales ledger control account	90,000
Less Irrecoverable debts	(4,400)
Adjusted balance per sales ledger control account	85,600
Less specific allowance	(1,300)
	84,300
General allowance (£84,300 × 4%)	3,372
∴ Total allowance:	
Specific	1,300
General	3,372
Total closing allowance	4,672
Calculating the allowance for doubtful debts – adjustments	
Opening allowance (per scenario)	1,600
Adjustment (to TB – SPL)	3,072
Closing allowance (to TB – SOFP)	4,672

Explanation:

The closing allowance (£4,672) is higher than the opening allowance (£1,600). Therefore, the allowance for doubtful debts – adjustment is an expense in the profit or loss account (£3,072) and would be a debit entry in the trial balance.

....

Task 8.6

Trial balance (extract)

Ledger account	Ledger balance	
	Debit £	Credit £
Sales ledger control account	184,000	
Irrecoverable debts	16,000	
Allowance for doubtful debts		6,620
Allowance for doubtful debts – adjustments		980

Working:

	£
Opening balance per sales ledger control account	200,000
Less Irrecoverable debts	(16,000)
Adjusted balance per sales ledger control account	184,000
Less specific allowance	(3,000)
	181,000
General allowance (£181,000 × 2%)	3,620
∴Total allowance:	
Specific	3,000
General	3,620
Total closing allowance	6,620
Calculating the allowance for doubtful debts – adjustments	
Opening allowance (per scenario)	7,600
Adjustment (to TB – SPL)	(980)
Closing allowance (to TB – SOFP)	6,620

Explanation:

The closing allowance (£6,620) is lower than the opening allowance (£7,600). Therefore, the allowance for doubtful debts – adjustment (£980) is a reduction in expenses in the profit or loss account and a credit entry in the trial balance.

•••

Task 8.7

	✓
Depreciation	
Inventory	
Accruals	✓
Prudence	

Explanation:

The allowance for doubtful debts is offset against the trade receivables balance in the statement of financial position, thereby achieving matching under the accruals basis of accounting.

•••

Chapter 9

Task 9.1

	Answer
A credit balance on the bank statement indicates a	**positive cash balance**
A credit balance on the cash book indicates a	**negative cash balance**

Explanation:

Statement 1: The bank statement is prepared from the bank's point of view. So if a customer has money in their account, the money is held by the bank but does not belong to the bank. Effectively, from the bank's perspective, it represents a liability to the customer. Therefore, a credit balance on the bank statement indicates a positive cash balance for the customer.

Statement 2: The cash book is prepared from the business's point of view. In accordance with the rules of double entry bookkeeping, a credit balance indicates a liability and therefore a negative cash balance.

••

Task 9.2

A positive cash balance is a **debit** entry in the cash book.

A negative cash balance is shown on the bank statement as a **debit** entry.

Explanation:

When a business has a negative cash balance, the bank shows this as a debit balance (D) on the bank statement. This is because from the bank's point of view, the business owes the bank money so the business is effectively the bank's receivable.

••

Task 9.3

Cash book as at 31 July

Date 20X2	Details	Bank £	Date 20X2	Cheque number	Details	Bank £
01 July	Balance b/d	8,751	11 July	103122	ENG	1,100
03 July	LKI	2,875	18 July	103123	JHP	158
14 July	ABW	6,351	27 July	103125	MWY	7,565
17 July	WNY	3,560	29 July	103126	YMN	4,320
28 July	OKM	8,590	13 July		Direct debit – Gas	4,895
			31 July		Balance c/d	12,089
		30,127				30,127
1 August	Balance b/d	12,089				

Bank reconciliation statement	£
Balance per bank statement	12,849
WNY	3,560
Total to add	
YMN	4,320
Total to subtract	
Balance as per cash book	12,089

Task 9.4

Adjustment	Amount £	Debit ✓	Credit ✓
Adjustment (1)	25		✓
Adjustment (3)	9	✓	
Adjustment (4)	2,827		✓

Explanation – cash book:

Narrative	Amount £
Unadjusted balance per cash book	3,851
Adjustment (1)	(25)
Adjustment (3)	9
Adjustment (4)	(2,827)
Adjusted balance per cash book	1,008

Explanation – bank statement:

Narrative	Amount £
Balance per bank statement	(778)
Outstanding lodgements (note 2)	1,738
Payment to supplier (note 5)	(452)
Bank error (note 6)	500
Balance as per the adjusted cash book	1,008

Task 9.5

Adjustment	Amount £	Debit ✓	Credit ✓
Adjustment (3)	996	✓	
Adjustment (4)	2,827		✓
Adjustment (6)	440		✓

Explanation – cash book:

Narrative	Amount £
Unadjusted balance per cash book	11,442
Adjustment (3)	996
Adjustment (4)	(2,827)
Adjustment (6)	(440)
Adjusted balance per cash book	9,171

Explanation – bank statement:

Narrative	Amount £
Balance per bank statement	7,377
Payment to supplier (note 1)	(990)
Outstanding lodgements (note 2)	3,560
Payment to supplier (note 5)	(776)
	9,171

Chapter 10

Task 10.1

Sales ledger control account

	£		£
Balance b/d	4,268	Sales returns	995
Sales	15,487	Irrecoverable debts	210
		Bank	13,486
		Discounts allowed	408
		Purchases ledger control account	150
		Balance c/d	4,506
	19,755		19,755

Task 10.2

Purchases ledger control account

	£		£
Bank	10,379	Balance b/d	3,299
Purchases returns	1,074	Purchases	12,376
Discounts received	302		
Sales ledger control account	230		
Balance c/d	3,690		
	15,675		15,675

Task 10.3

Adjustment	Amount £	Debit ✓	Credit ✓
Adjustment (3)	3,300		✓
Adjustment (4)	1,000	✓	
Adjustment (6)	840		✓

Explanation – subsidiary sales ledger balances:

Narrative	Amount £
Per scenario:	6,310
Adjustment (1)	(460)
Adjustment (2)	(250)
Adjustment (5) (£680 × 2)	(1,360)
Adjusted subsidiary sales ledger balance:	4,240

Explanation – sales ledger control account:

Narrative	Amount £
Per scenario:	7,380
Adjustment (3) (£1,650 × 2)	(3,300)
Adjustment (4)	1,000
Adjustment (6)	(840)
Adjusted sales ledger control account balance:	4,240

Task 10.4

Adjustment	Amount £	Debit ✓	Credit ✓
Adjustment (1)	100	✓	
Adjustment (4)	1,140	✓	
Adjustment (5)	1,360		✓

Explanation – subsidiary sales ledger balances:

Narrative	Amount £
Per scenario:	6,100
Adjustment (1)	100
Adjustment (4) (£570 × 2)	1,140
Adjustment (5) (£680 × 2)	(1,360)
Adjusted subsidiary sales ledger balance:	5,980

Explanation – sales ledger control account:

Narrative	Amount £
Per scenario:	11,840
Adjustment (2)	(3,000)
Adjustment (3)	(2,400)
Adjustment (6)	(460)
Adjusted sales ledger control account balance:	5,980

Task 10.5

Adjustment	Amount £	Debit ✓	Credit ✓
Adjustment (2)	850	✓	
Adjustment (3)	72	✓	
Adjustment (6)	1,329	✓	

Explanation – subsidiary purchases ledger balances:

Narrative	Amount £
Per scenario:	2,219
Adjustment (4)	(214)
Adjustment (5) (£403 × 2)	(806)
Adjusted subsidiary purchases ledger balance:	1,199

Note. Adjustment 1 does not change the total of the subsidiary purchases ledger balances.

Explanation – purchases ledger control account:

Narrative	Amount £
Per scenario:	3,450
Adjustment (2)	(850)
Adjustment (3) (£791 – £719)	(72)
Adjustment (6)	(1,329)
Adjusted purchases ledger control account balance:	1,199

Task 10.6

Adjustment	Amount £	Debit ✓	Credit ✓
Adjustment (3)	1,320		✓
Adjustment (4)	1,210	✓	
Adjustment (6)	1,240	✓	

Explanation – subsidiary purchases ledger balances:

Narrative	Amount £
Per scenario:	8,670
Adjustment (3) (£660 × 2)	1,320
Adjustment (4)	(1,210)
Adjustment (6) (£620 × 2)	(1,240)
Adjusted subsidiary purchases ledger balance:	7,540

Explanation – purchases ledger control account:

Narrative	Amount £
Per scenario:	5,248
Adjustment (1)	(980)
Adjustment (2)	3,592
Adjustment (5)	(320)
Adjusted purchases ledger control account balance:	7,540

BPP
LEARNING MEDIA

Task 10.7

(a)

	£
Balance on supplier's statement of account	3,475
Balance on supplier's account in Magenta's purchases ledger *(£500 + £1,750 + £925) – (£420 + £530)	2,225
Difference (£3,475 – £2,225) *	1,250

* Calculations are included for tutorial purposes and do not form part of the answer.

Explanation:

To work out the balance on the supplier's account in the purchases ledger, add up the amounts on each side of the supplier's account and find the balance as a missing figure on the side with the lower total. Remember that everything on the left side of the account reduces the total owed to the supplier, and everything on the right side of the account increases the total owed to the supplier.

(b)

	✓
Cheque for £420	
Invoice number 147	
Credit note number 23	
Invoice number 178	
Invoice number 195	✓

Explanation:

The best way to approach part (b) is to work through the statement of account and tick off each item that also appears in the purchases ledger. The unticked items remaining will enable you to answer part (b). Ignore the brought forward balance on the statement of account for the purposes of the ticking exercise.

Note that the difference identified in part (a) of £1,250 is the amount of the missing invoice 195 identified in part (b). This is a good way to check that the reconciliation is accurate.

Task 10.8

(a)

Account name	Amount £	Debit ✓	Credit ✓
Wages expense	128,000	✓	
Wages control account	128,000		✓

Working: £120,000 + £8,000 = £128,000

(b)

Account name	Amount £	Debit ✓	Credit ✓
Wages control account	28,000	✓	
HM Revenue and Customs	28,000		✓

Working: £4,000 + £16,000 + £8,000 = £28,000

(c)

Account name	Amount £	Debit ✓	Credit ✓
Wages control account	100,000	✓	
Bank	100,000		✓

Working: £120,000 – £16,000 – £4,000 = £100,000

Remember, the employer's NI of £8,000 is not deducted from the gross pay. It is an additional amount paid by the employer to HMRC.

Chapter 11

Task 11.1

Description	Type of error	Balancing trial balance?
A debit entry has been posted with no corresponding credit made.	Single entry error	No
An entry has been made so that debits equal credits but the amount is incorrect.	Error of original entry	Yes
A transaction has been recorded at the correct amount but the debit and credit entries have been reversed.	Reversal of entries	Yes
Debits equal credits; however, one of the entries has been made to the wrong type of account.	Error of principle	Yes

Task 11.2

Error	Imbalance ✓	No imbalance ✓
The payment of the telephone bill was posted to the cash book – credit side and then credited to the telephone account.	✓	
The depreciation expense was debited to the accumulated depreciation account and credited to the depreciation charges account.		✓
The electricity account balance of £750 was taken to the trial balance as £570.	✓	
The motor expenses were debited to the motor vehicles at cost account. The credit entry is correct.		✓
Discounts received were not posted to the general ledger.		✓

Task 11.3

		Debit balance ✓	Credit balance ✓
£	8,304		✓

Task 11.4

(a)

Account name	Debit £	Credit £
Telephone	236	
Electricity		236

(b)

Account name	Debit £	Credit £
Sales ledger control account	180	
Sales		180

(c)

Account name	Debit £	Credit £
Purchases ledger control account	38	
Purchases returns		38

Task 11.5

(a)

Account name	Debit £	Credit £
Allowance for doubtful debts – adjustments	254	
Allowance for doubtful debts		254

Explanation:

The correction is twice the original error (£127 × 2 = £254)

(b)

Account name	Debit £	Credit £
Purchases ledger control account	400	
Sales ledger control account		400

Explanation:

The correction is twice the original error (£200 × 2 = £400)

(c)

Account name	Debit £	Credit £
Irrecoverable debts	680	
Sales ledger control account		680

Task 11.6

(a)

£	6,480

Working:

£32,400 (from the trial balance) × 20% = £6,480.

(b) **Extract from the extended trial balance**

Ledger account	Ledger balances		Adjustments	
	Debit £	Credit £	Debit £	Credit £
Bank	5,321			140
Carriage outwards			460	
Depreciation charges			6,480	
Irrecoverable debts	632			
Office expenses	52,832		140	
Plant at cost	32,400			
Plant accumulated depreciation		6,480		6,480
Prepaid expenses	305			
Purchases	89,430			890
Purchases ledger control account		11,230		
Rent	12,520			
Sales		104,502		
Sales ledger control account	16,230			
Suspense		430	890	460
VAT		9,320		

Workings:

Offices expenses: £70 × 2 = £140

Purchases balance: £89,430 – £88,540 = £890

Task 11.7

(a)

£	14

Working:

	£
Balance per the sales ledger control account	18,200
Closing allowance for doubtful debts (£18,200 × 2%)	364
Opening allowance for doubtful debts (per TB)	(350)
Allowance for doubtful debts adjustment	14

Extract from the extended trial balance

Ledger account	Ledger balances		Adjustments	
	Debit £	Credit £	Debit £	Credit £
Allowance for doubtful debts		350		14
Allowance for doubtful debts – adjustments			14	
Accrued expenses		750		
Bank		6,320	12,640	
Carriage inwards	219			
Closing inventory			8,430	8,430
Depreciation charges	6,625			
Discounts allowed	620			
Office expenses	488			
Opening inventory	4,420			
Prepaid expenses	305			
Purchases	89,430			
Purchases returns				560
Purchases ledger control account		11,230		
Sales		104,502		
Sales ledger control account	18,200			
Suspense	12,080		560	12,640

Explanation:

Bank entry: £6,320 × 2 = £12,640

£6,320 removes the error and then £6,320 includes bank on the correct side of the extended trial balance. In respect of the bank error, this removes the suspense account entry.

....

Task 11.8

	✓
A decrease in the allowance for doubtful debts from 3% of outstanding trade receivables to 2% of outstanding trade receivables	✓
The write down of an item of inventory which cost £1,500 and had a selling price of £1,350 and expected selling costs of £200	
Recognising an accrual for vehicle running expenses for September 20X6 but not invoiced and paid until October 20X6	
Decreasing the useful life of a computer with effect from the start of the year (1 October 20X5)	

Explanation:

The double entry to record a decrease in allowance for doubtful debts is:

Debit Allowance for doubtful debts (SOFP)

Credit Allowance for doubtful debts – adjustments (SPL)

The credit of this double entry results in an increase in profit, making this the correct answer. All of the other adjustments result in a decrease in profit:

Write down of inventory of £350 (£1,500 – [£1,350 – £200]):

Debit Closing inventory – statement of profit or loss   £350
Credit Closing inventory – statement of financial position   £350

Recognising an accrual:

Debit Vehicle running expenses (SPL)

Credit Accrued expenses (SOFP)

Decreasing the useful life of a computer would increase the depreciation expense and therefore reduce the profit:

Debit Depreciation charges (SPL)

Credit Accumulated depreciation (SOFP)

....

Task 11.9

	✓
Complete the accounts without any further adjustment, as any change could affect the outcome of the meeting with the bank.	
Complete the accounts without any further adjustment because the client's needs must take priority.	
Explain to the managing partner that you have discovered an irrecoverable debt which needs writing off because the accounts must be prepared in accordance with International Financial Reporting Standards.	✓
Write off the irrecoverable debt without telling your managing partner as you want to make sure that you get the pay rise that he's promised you.	

Explanation:

As a trainee accounting technician, we are bound by the *AAT's Code of Professional Ethics*. If we were to ignore the potential adjustment for the irrecoverable debt, we would not be complying with the fundamental principle of professional competence as the accounts would not be prepared in accordance with accounting standards.

There is a familiarity threat here due to the relationship between the proprietor and the managing partner and a potential intimidation threat arising from the possible loss of pay rise if the managing partner's wishes are not followed. So the only acceptable treatment is to try and persuade the managing partner of the need to adjust for the irrecoverable debt.

....

Task 11.10

	✓
Do nothing because the cash sales were accurately recorded in the cash book.	
Seek advice from the managing partner as it is possible that these sales were deliberately created with the intention of increasing profit for the year ended 30 June 20X3 and are not a genuine business transaction.	✓
Ignore the discovery because the client is a good friend and you trust him implicitly.	
Insist that the client reverses these sales and threaten to resign because it is clear that there has deliberately overstated the profit.	

Explanation:

As an AAT trainee accounting technician, we need to be aware of the effects including misleading period end adjustments. They could, for example, result in misinformed decision-making by users of the final accounts. These sales look suspicious because they were created on the last day of the year and then reversed on the first day of the following accounting period. Therefore, even if the client is a good friend, we have a duty to investigate this and as a trainee, it would be best to approach the managing partner for advice on how to proceed.

Task 11.11

	✓
It is a memorandum account to keep track of amounts owing from individual customers and owed to individual suppliers.	
It will detect all bookkeeping errors.	
It is prepared after closing off the general ledger accounts and before preparing the final accounts.	✓
It will always include a suspense account.	

Explanation:

The trial balance lists the closing balances on each general ledger account. The balances are listed on the debit or credit side as appropriate. It is an important step in the preparation of the final accounts.

It is not a memorandum account showing amounts owing from individual customers or owed to individual suppliers; this is a description of the purchases and sales ledgers.

It will not detect every error as some errors allow the trial balance to balance.

It only includes a suspense account if it does not initially balance; it will not always include a suspense account.

....

Task 11.12

(a)

Account	Debit £	Credit £
Depreciation expense	1,056	
Fixtures and fittings accumulated depreciation		1,056

(b)

Account	Debit £	Credit £
Suspense	120	
Accruals		120

(c)

Account	Debit £	Credit £
Closing inventory – statement of financial position	8,255	
Closing inventory – statement of profit or loss		8,255

Workings:

Inventory should be valued at the lower of cost (£445) and NRV (£250) so a write down of £195 is required (£445 – £250).

This reduces total closing inventory to £8,255 (£8,450 – £195).

(d)

Account	Debit £	Credit £
Suspense	1,774	
Purchase returns		1,774

Workings:

Should have done		Did do		Correction	
DR PLCA	£887	DR PLCA	£887	DR Suspense	£1,774
CR Purchases returns	£887	DR Purchases returns	£887	CR Purchase returns £1,774	
		CR Suspense	£1,774		

(e) **Complete the following sentence:**

| I cannot | conclude that the balances included are now free from all errors.

| I can | conclude that the debit and credit sides of the trial balance will be equal.

....

Chapter 12

Task 12.1

(a) An extended trial balance is an accounting technique of moving from the [initial] trial balance, through the year end adjustments, to the figures for the [final] accounts.

(b) When an extended trial balance is extended and a business has made a profit, this figure for profit will be in the [debit] column of the statement of profit or loss.

••

Task 12.2

Statements	✓
The balance on the suspense account should appear on the debit side of the statement of profit or loss columns.	
The balance on the suspense account should appear on the credit side of the statement of financial position columns.	
The balance on the suspense account should not appear in the statement of profit or loss or the statement of financial position columns in the extended trial balance.	✓

••

Task 12.3
Extended trial balance

Ledger account	Statement of profit or loss		Statement of financial position	
	Debit ✓	Credit ✓	Debit ✓	Credit ✓
Allowance for doubtful debts				✓
Allowance for doubtful debts – adjustment (increase in allowance)	✓			
Bank overdraft				✓
Capital				✓
Closing inventory		✓	✓	
Depreciation charges	✓			
Purchases returns		✓		
Opening inventory	✓			
VAT owed from HMRC			✓	

Explanation:

In this task, the following should be noted:

- The allowance for doubtful debts – adjustment is an increase in the allowance. This results in an expense. Therefore, it is shown on the debit side of the statement of profit or loss columns.

- The bank has an overdraft and therefore is a liability. For this reason, it is included in the statement of financial position credit column.

- The VAT is owed from HMRC. This means it is an asset and so it is shown in the statement of financial position debit column.

Task 12.4

Extended trial balance

Ledger account	Ledger balances		Adjustments		Statement of profit or loss		Statement of financial position	
	Debit £	Credit £	Debit £	Credit £	Debit £	Credit £	Debit £	Credit £
Allowance for doubtful debts		2,380	420					1,960
Allowance for doubtful debts – adjustment	1,600			420	1,180			
Bank	2,400		230				2,630	
Capital		25,800						25,800
Closing inventory			13,500	13,500		13,500	13,500	
Depreciation charges	9,203		4,000		13,203			
Office expenses	600				600			
Opening inventory	2,560				2,560			
Payroll expenses	16,400				16,400			
Purchases	22,400				22,400			
Purchases ledger control account		8,900	300					8,600
Sales		45,150		60		45,210		
Sales ledger control account	11,205			300			10,905	
Selling expenses	1,700				1,700			
Suspense	170		60	230				
VAT		12,000						12,000
Vehicles at cost	64,192						64,192	
Vehicles accumulated depreciation		38,200		4,000				42,200
Profit for the year					667			667
Total	132,430	132,430	18,510	18,510	**58,710**	**58,710**	**91,227**	**91,227**

Explanation:

In this task, the following should be noted:

The allowance for doubtful debts – adjustment is in the statement of profit or loss debit column. This shows that the allowance for doubtful debts is higher at the end of this year than at the end of the previous period.

The VAT balance of £12,000 is entered in the credit column of the statement of financial position. This shows it is an amount due to HMRC and a liability.

By adding across the suspense account row, this account is cleared to zero, as is expected after all year end adjustments have been posted.

Having extended the figures into the statement of profit or loss columns, adding down, the credit side is the higher of the two columns (£58,710). Before adjustment the statement of profit or loss debit column is only £58,043. Therefore, by including a 'Profit for the year' figure of £667 in the final row of the debit column, the two columns balance. To complete the double entry, £667 is recorded in the statement of financial position credit column.

All pairs of columns now balance. As the £667 is in the statement of profit or loss debit column and statement of financial position credit column, this shows that the business has generated a profit for the year.

Task 12.5

Extended trial balance

Ledger account	Ledger balances Debit £	Ledger balances Credit £	Adjustments Debit £	Adjustments Credit £	Statement of profit or loss Debit £	Statement of profit or loss Credit £	Statement of financial position Debit £	Statement of financial position Credit £
Bank		4,123		4,235				8,358
Capital		20,000						20,000
Closing inventory			3,414	3,414		3,414	3,414	
Depreciation charges	2,415		1,352		3,767			
Irrecoverable debts	124				124			
Loan		10,000						10,000
Machine at cost	51,600						51,600	
Machine accumulated depreciation		13,210		1,352				14,562
Opening inventory	6,116				6,116			
Prepaid expenses	215		352				567	
Purchases	39,321		519		39,840			
Purchases ledger control account		13,421						13,421
Purchases returns		299		519		818		
Sales		72,032		511		72,543		
Sales ledger control account	38,597			3,770			34,827	
Sales returns	2,057		511		2,568			
Suspense		3,418	3,770	352				
VAT		3,942	4,235				293	
Profit for the year					24,360			24,360
Total	140,445	140,445	14,153	14,153	76,775	76,775	90,701	90,701

Explanation:

In this task, the following should be noted:

The bank balance of £8,358 is an overdraft and therefore in the statement of financial position credit column.

The VAT balance of £293 is money owed from HMRC (being the difference between a credit balance £3,942 and a debit balance of £4,235). It is entered in the debit column of the statement of financial position.

By adding across the suspense account row, this account is cleared to zero, as is expected after all year end adjustments have been posted.

Having extended the figures into the statement of profit or loss columns, adding down, the credit side is the higher of the two columns (£76,775). Before adjustment the statement of profit or loss debit column is only £52,415. Therefore, by including a 'Profit for the year' figure of £24,360 in the final row of the debit column, the two columns balance. To complete the double entry, £24,360 is recorded in the statement of financial position credit column.

All pairs of columns now balance. As the £24,360 is in the statement of profit or loss debit column and statement of financial position credit column, this shows that the business has generated a profit for the year.

••

AAT AQ2016 SAMPLE ASSESSMENT 1
ADVANCED BOOKKEEPING

Time allowed: 2 hours

The AAT may call the assessments on their website, under study support resources, either a 'practice assessment' or 'sample assessment'.

Advanced Bookkeeping (AVBK)
AAT sample assessment 1

Task 1 (21 marks)

This task is about non-current assets.

You are working on the accounting records of a business known as AMBR Trading.

You may ignore VAT in this task.

The following is an extract from a purchase invoice received by AMBR Trading relating to new equipment for its commercial kitchen:

To: AMBR Trading Unit 6, East End Trading Estate Southgrove HS14 6PW	Invoice 965270 Katerkit Ltd Cator Way Gatebury TY6 5VB	Date: 01 April 20X6
Item	**Details**	**£**
Electric combi-steam oven	CSO31	5,565.00
Colour touch control display	For CSO31	999.00
Floor stand	For CSO31	224.00
Electric portable pasta boiler	PSB69	245.00
Net total		7,033.00

The acquisition has been made under a finance lease agreement.

The following information relates to the sale of some computer equipment no longer used by the business:

Item description	Desktop DTC3
Date of sale	31 December 20X6
Selling price	£180.00

- AMBR Trading has a policy of capitalising expenditure over £500.

- Kitchen equipment is depreciated at 20% per year on a diminishing balance basis.

- Computer equipment is depreciated over four years on a straight line basis assuming no residual value.

- Depreciation is calculated on an annual basis and charged in equal instalments for each full month an asset is owned in the year.

(a) **For the year ended 31 March 20X7, record the following in the extract from the non-current assets register below:**

- **Any acquisition of non-current assets**
- **Any disposals of non-current assets**
- **Depreciation.**

Note. Not every cell will acquire an entry.

Show your numerical answers to TWO decimal places.

Use the DD/MM/YY format for any dates.

Use the drop-down list below to select your answers where indicated, otherwise enter the number or date into the relevant cell.

Extract from non-current assets register

Description/ Serial number	Acquisition date	Cost £	Depreciation charges £	Carrying amount £	Funding method	Disposal proceeds £	Disposal date
Kitchen equipment							
Double-door freezer DDF4	01/04/X4	1,995.00			Part-exchange		
Year end 31/03/X5			399.00	1,596.00			
Year end 31/03/X6			319.20	1,276.80			
Year end 31/03/X7							
▼					▼		
Year end 31/03/X7							
Computer equipment							
Restaurant POS tablet bundle	01/10/X4	1,380.00			Hire purchase		
Year end 31/03/X5			172.50	1,207.50			
Year end 31/03/X6			345.00	862.50			

206

Description/ Serial number	Acquisition date	Cost £	Depreciation charges £	Carrying amount £	Funding method	Disposal proceeds £	Disposal date
Year end 31/03/X7				517.50			
Desktop DTC3	01/01/X5	579.84			Cash		
Year end 31/03/X5			36.24	543.60			
Year end 31/03/X6			144.96	398.64			
Year end 31/03/X7			▾	▾			

Drop-down list:

Desktop DTC3	0.00	0.00	Cash
Freezer DDF4	99.66	253.68	Finance lease
Electric oven CSO31	108.72	289.92	Hire purchase
Pasta boiler PSB69	144.96	298.98	

(b)   Complete the following sentences.

It is important to obtain prior authority for capital expenditure in order

[▾]

The bank manager [▾] be the appropriate person to give this authority.

Drop-down list:

to achieve the appropriate level of materiality.
to comply with international financial reporting standards.
to ensure that the business as a whole will benefit from the purchase.

would
would not

....

Task 2 (17 marks)

This task is about ledger accounting for non-current assets.

- You are working on the accounting records of a business for the year ended 31 March 20X7. VAT can be ignored.

- A new vehicle has been acquired. It is estimated it will be used for four years.

- The cost was £12,448; this was paid from the bank.

- The business plans to sell the vehicle after four years when its residual value is expected to be £4,000.

- Vehicles are depreciated on a straight line basis. A full year's depreciation is applied in the year of acquisition.

- Depreciation has already been entered into the accounting records for existing vehicles.

(a) **Calculate the depreciation charge for the year on the new vehicle.**

£	

Make entries in the accounts below for:

- **The acquisition of the new vehicle**
- **The depreciation charge on the new vehicle**

On each account, show clearly the balance to be carried down or transferred to the statement of profit or loss, as appropriate.

Vehicle at cost

	£			£
Balance b/d	46,300		▼	
▼			▼	
▼			▼	

Depreciation charges

	£			£
Balance b/d	7,575		▼	
▼			▼	
▼				

Vehicles accumulated depreciation

	£		£
▼		Balance c/d	15,150
▼		▼	
▼		▼	

Drop-down list:

Balance b/d
Balance c/d
Bank
Depreciation charges
Disposals
Profit or loss account
Purchases
Purchases ledger control account
Sales
Sales ledger control account
Vehicle running expenses
Vehicle accumulated depreciation
Vehicles at cost
Empty

The business sold an item of office equipment which originally cost £1,800. The proceeds of £600 were paid into the bank:

(b) Insert the account names to the debit and credit columns to show where the entries for the proceeds will be made.

Debit	Credit

Disposals

Office equipment at cost

Bank

(c) **Show the journal entries required to remove the original cost of the equipment for the general ledger.**

Account		Amount £	Debit	Credit
	▼			
	▼			

Drop-down list:

Bank
Depreciation charges
Disposals
Office equipment accumulated depreciation
Office equipment at cost
Profit and loss account
Purchases
Purchases ledger control account
Sales
Sales ledger control account
Sales returns
Suspense
Vehicles accumulated depreciation
Vehicles at cost
Empty

....

Task 3 (19 marks)

This task is about ledger accounting, including accruals and prepayments, and applying ethical principles.

(a) **Enter the figures given in the table below in the appropriate trial balance columns.**

Do not enter zeros in unused column cells. Do not enter any figures as negatives.

Extract from the trial balance as at 31 March 20X7

Account	Ledger balance	Trial balance	
		Debit	Credit
	£	£	£
Accrued expenses	850		
Carriage inwards	2,240		
Discounts allowed	1,420		
Prepaid income	975		

You are working on the accounting records of a business for the year ended 31 March 20X7.

In this task, you can ignore VAT.

Business policy: accounting accruals and prepayments

An entry is made into the income or expense account and an opposite entry into the relevant asset or liability account. In the following period, this entry is removed.

You are looking at vehicle running expenses for the year.

- The cash book for the year shows payments for vehicle running expenses of £9,468.

- This includes the following payments for road fund licenses.

Road fund licenses for the period:	£
1 January – 31 December 20X7	516
1 April 20X7 – 31 March 20X8	405

(b) Calculate the value of the adjustment required for vehicle running expenses as at 31 March 20X7.

£ [   ]

Update the vehicles running expenses account. Show clearly:

- the cash book figure
- the year end adjustment
- the transfer to the statement of profit or loss for the year

Vehicle running expenses

	£		£
Prepaid expenses (reversal)	840	▼	
▼		▼	
▼		▼	

Drop-down list:

Accrued expenses
Accrued income
Balance b/d
Balance c/d
Bank
Commission income
Prepaid expenses
Prepaid income
Profit or loss account
Purchases
Purchases ledger control account
Sales
Sales ledger control account
Statement of financial position
Vehicle running expenses
Empty

You are now looking at commission income for the year.

Commission income of £2,070 was accrued on 31 March 20X6.

(c) **Complete the following statements:**

The reversal of this accrual is dated [▼] .

The reversal is on the [▼] side of the commission income account.

Drop-down list:

31 March 20X6
1 April 20X6
1 April 20X7

credit
debit

- The cash book for the year shows receipts for commission income of £42,805.
- Commission of £1,960 for the month ended 31 March 20X7 was received into the bank on 15 April 20X7.

(d) **Taking into account all the information you have, calculate the commission income for the year ended 31 March 20X7.**

£ [   ]

Your junior colleague asks why you are considering the receipt dated 15 April.

She is confused as the financial year ended on 31 March.

(e) **Which of the following can you use in your explanation to her?**

You must choose ONE answer for each row.

Reason for considering the receipt dated 15 April	Acceptable reason	Not acceptable reason
The proprietor of the business asked you to increase the profit for the year ended 31 March 20X7.		
The transaction is an expense relevant to the period ended 31 March 20X7.		
The figure is a current asset as at 31 March 20X7.		

Task 4 (23 marks)

This task is about accounting adjustments.

You are a trainee accounting technician reporting to a managing partner in an accounting practice. You are working on the accounting records of a business client.

A trial balance has been drawn up and balanced using a suspense account. You now need to make some corrections and adjustments for the year ended 31 March 20X7.

You may ignore VAT in this task.

The allowance for doubtful debts needs to be adjusted to 1% of the outstanding trade receivables.

(a)   Calculate the value of the adjustment required.

(b)   (i)   Record this adjustment into the extract from the extended trial balance below.

(ii)   Make the following further adjustments.

You will NOT need to enter adjustments on every line. Do NOT enter zeros into unused cells.

- Purchases of £984 have been posted to the office expenses account in error.

- A prepayment of £450 for airfares has been posted correctly on the credit side. There was no corresponding debit entry. These costs are classified as sales expenses.

- The plant as cost account in the general ledger correctly shows a balance of £24,500. This has been incorrectly transferred to the final balances as £25,400.

Extract from the extended trial balance

Ledger account	Ledger balances		Adjustments	
	Debit £	Credit £	Debit £	Credit £
Allowance for doubtful debts		225		
Allowance for doubtful debts – adjustments				
Bank	2,815			
Irrecoverable debts	390			
Office expenses	116,310			
Plant at cost	25,400			
Plant accumulated depreciation		12,250		
Prepaid expenses	505			
Purchases	108,265			
Purchases ledger control account		9,622		
Rent	14,800			
Sales		188,748		
Sales expenses	8,606			
Sales ledger control account	17,900			
Suspense		450		

(c) **Show the journal entries that will be required to close off the rent account for the financial year end and select an appropriate narrative.**

Journal

		Dr £	Cr £
	▼		
	▼		

Narrative:

	▼

Drop-down list:

Allowance for doubtful debts
Allowance for doubtful debts – adjustment
Bank
Irrecoverable debts
Office expenses
Plant accumulated depreciation
Plant at cost
Prepaid expenses
Profit of loss account
Purchases ledger control account
Rent
Sales
Sales expenses
Sales ledger control account
Statement of financial position
Suspense
Empty

Closure of general ledger for the year ended 31 March 20X7
Closure of rent account to the suspense account
Transfer of rent for year ended 31 March 20X7 to the statement of financial position
Transfer of rent for year ended 31 March 20X7 to the profit or loss account

Your manager has now reviewed the resulting figures in the draft accounts. He is concerned that the client may have significantly understated the irrecoverable debt figures and this will need further investigation. You know that the client is pressuring to get the final accounts completed for what she describes as an important meeting for the future of the business. Any further investigation will mean her deadline cannot be met.

(d) **What should you and your manager do next, and why? Choose ONE.**

	✓
Investigate the collectability of debts and delay completion of the accounts, as any adjustment could affect the outcome of the meeting.	
Investigate the collectability of debts and delay completion of the accounts because the client will have overstated the importance of the meeting.	
Complete the accounts by the deadline without any further adjustment, as any change is unlikely to be relevant to the meeting.	
Complete the accounts by the deadline without any further adjustment because the client's needs must take priority.	

Task 5 (20 marks)

This task is about period end routines using accounting, records and the extended trial balance.

You are preparing the bank reconciliation for a sole trader.

The balance showing on the bank statement is a debt of £1,930 and the balance in the cash book is a debit of £2,407.

The bank statement has been compared with the cash book at 31 March and the following points noted.

1. A remittance advice from a customer has been received and an entry made in the cash book for the correct amount of £734. This is not yet showing on the bank statement.

2. A cheque from a customer for £367 for a debt outstanding at the year end was received in April 20X7.

3. A faster payment of £2,174 for the purchase of a non-current asset is showing on the bank statement but has not been entered in the accounting records.

4. The bank has made an error. On the last day of the month, a payment of £1,087 on the statement was duplicated.

5. A direct debit payment of £422 has been recorded in the accounts as £222.

6. Interest charges of £142 have not been entered in the cash book.

(a) Use the following table to show the THREE items that should appear on the cash book side of the reconciliation. Enter only ONE figure for each line. Do not enter zeros in unused cells.

Adjustment		Debit £	Credit £
▼			
▼			
▼			

Drop-down list:

Adjustment 1
Adjustment 2
Adjustment 3
Adjustment 4
Adjustment 5
Adjustment 6
Empty

(b) **Which of the following statements about the net pay control account is TRUE? Choose ONE.**

The net pay control account...

	✓
...is a summary of memorandum accounts for each employee.	
...should have a balance of zero when all relevant entries have been correctly made.	
...will always be accurate when the bank reconciliation has been completed.	
...should include individual entries for gross pay due to each employee.	

You are now working on the accounting records of a different business.

You have the following extended trial balance. The adjustments have already been correctly entered.

(c) **Extend the figures into the statement of profit or loss and statement of financial position columns.**

Do NOT enter zeros into unused column cells.

Complete the extended trial balance by entering figures and a label in the correct places.

Drop-down list:

Profit/loss for the year
Suspense
Balance b/d
Balance c/d
Gross profit/loss for the year

Extended trial balance

Ledger account	Ledger balances		Adjustments		Statement of profit or loss		Statement of financial position	
	Debit £	Credit £	Debit £	Credit £	Debit £	Credit £	Debit £	Credit £
Bank		958		75				
Capital		11,000						
Closing inventory			9,930	9,930				
Depreciation charges	3,895							
Equipment at cost	20,162			689				
Equipment accumulated depreciation		15,579						
Interest paid	63		75					
Loan		6,566	1,085					
Office expenses	22,495		689	290				
Opening inventory	10,058							
Payroll expenses	20,825							
Prepayments			290					
Purchases	79,454							
Purchases ledger control account		13,167						
Sales		126,139		485				
Sales ledger control account	16,979							
Suspense	600		485	1,085				
VAT		1,122						
▼								
Total	174,531	174,531	12,554	12,554				

AAT AQ2016 SAMPLE ASSESSMENT 1 ADVANCED BOOKKEEPING

ANSWERS

Advanced Bookkeeping (AVBK)
AAT sample assessment 1

Task 1 (21 marks)

(a) For the year ended 31 March 20X7, record the following in the extract from the non-current assets register below:

- Any acquisitions of non-current assets
- Any disposals of non-current assets
- Depreciation

Description/ Serial number	Acquisition date	Cost £	Depreciation charges £	Carrying amount £	Funding method	Disposal proceeds £	Disposal date
Kitchen equipment							
Double-door freezer DDF4	01/04/X4	1,995.00			Part-exchange		
Year end 31/03/X5			399.00	1,596.00			
Year end 31/03/X6			319.20	1,276.80			
Year end 31/03/X7			**255.36**	**1,021.44**			
Electric oven CSO31	01/04/X6	6,788.00			Finance lease		
Year end 31/03/X7			**1,357.60**	**5,430.40**			
Computer equipment							
Restaurant POS tablet bundle	01/10/X4	1,380.00			Hire purchase		
Year end 31/03/X5			172.50	1,207.50			
Year end 31/03/X6			345.00	862.50			
Year end 31/03/X7			**345.00**	**517.50**			

223

Description/ Serial number	Acquisition date	Cost £	Depreciation charges £	Carrying amount £	Funding method	Disposal proceeds £	Disposal date
Desktop DTC3	01/01/X5	579.84			Cash		
Year end 31/03/X5			36.24	543.60			
Year end 31/03/X6			144.96	398.64			
Year end 31/03/X7			**108.72**	**0.00**		**180.00**	**31/12/X6**

Workings:

Kitchen Equipment depreciation

1276.80 × 20% = 255.36 (carrying value multiplied by the rate of depreciation) = 255.36

Electric oven CSO31

The cost is calculated as 5,565.00 (the oven) + 999.00 (the control display) + 224.00 (the floor stand) = 6.788. This is because all of these costs relate to the oven. The pasta boiler is a separate asset and falls below the £500 capitalisation threshold so should be recorded as an expense rather than an asset.

Depreciation = 6,788 × 20% = 1,357.60

Computer equipment (Restaurant POS tablet bundle) is depreciated on a straight line basis, therefore, the charge for year ended 31/3/07 is the same as the previous year (1380/4 = 345). The first year's depreciation was apportioned for the number of months of ownership in the year of acquisition.

Desktop DTC3 was disposed of in year ended 31/3/X7, so the depreciation in that final year has been apportioned accordingly:

579.84/4 = 144.96 (full year depreciation)

144.96/12 months × 9 months (disposed of 31 December) = 108.72

(b) **Complete the following sentences.**

It is important to obtain prior authority for capital expenditure in order

to ensure that the business as a whole will benefit from the purchase .

The bank manager would not be the appropriate person to give this authority.

Explanation:

Capital purchases should be considered as to whether they will benefit the company, in terms of generating revenues, improving efficiencies or supporting the production of new product lines.

The decision to buy a new capital asset would not be affected by the international reporting standards (although how the purchase is recorded in the financial statements **would** be considered) and the question of materiality would only arise when the auditors look at the financial statements.

The bank manager is not an official within the company and therefore would not be the most appropriate person to approve the purchase.

Task 2 (17 marks)

(a) **Calculate the depreciation charge for the year on the new vehicle.**

£	2,112

Workings:

$$\frac{£12,448 - £4,000}{4 \text{ years}} = £2,112$$

No apportionment as a full year charge in year of acquisition.

Make entries in the accounts below for:

- **The acquisition of the new vehicle**
- **The depreciation charge on the new vehicle**

Vehicle at cost

	£		£
Balance b/d	46,300	Balance c/d	58,748
Bank	12,448		
	58,748		58,748

Depreciation charges

	£		£
Balance b/d	7,575	Profit or loss account	9,687
Vehicles accumulated depreciation	2,112		
	9,687		9,687

Vehicles accumulated depreciation

	£		£
Balance c/d	17,262	Balance b/d	15,150
		Depreciation charges	2,112
	17,262		17,262

(b) Insert the account names to the debit and credit columns to show where the entries for the proceeds will be made.

Debit	Credit
Bank	Disposals

(c) Show the journal entries required to remove the original cost of the equipment from the general ledger.

Account	Amount £	Debit	Credit
Disposals	1,800	✓	
Office equipment at cost	1,800		✓

Task 3 (19 marks)

(a) **Enter the figures given in the table below in the appropriate trial balance columns.**

Do not enter zeros in unused column cells. Do not enter any figures as negatives.

Extract from the trial balance as at 31 March 20X7

Account	Ledger balance	Trial balance	
	£	£ Dr	£ Cr
Accrued expenses	850		850
Carriage inwards	2,240	2,240	
Discounts allowed	1,420	1,420	
Prepaid income	975		975

(b) **Calculate the value of the adjustment required for vehicle running expenses as at 31 March 20X7.**

£	–792

Workings:

Year end is 31 March 20X7

Apportion the road licences to cover any period after 1 April X7 as being prepaid for the next period (needs to be removed from current year's expenses):

1 Jan-31 Dec 20X7= £516 × 9/12   =   387
1 Apr 20X7 – 31 March 20X8   =   405 (100% next period cost)
Adjustment   792

Update the vehicles running expenses account. Show clearly:

- **The cash book figure**
- **The year end adjustment**
- **The transfer to the statement of profit or loss for the year**

Vehicle running expenses

	£		£
Prepaid expenses (reversal)	840	Prepaid expenses	792
Bank	9,468	Profit or loss account	9,516
	10,308		10,308

(c) Complete the following statements:

The reversal of this accrual is dated | 1 April 20X6 | .

The reversal is on the | debit | side of the commission income account.

(d) Taking into account all the information you have, calculate the commission income for the year ended 31 March 20X7.

£ | 42,695

Workings:

	£
Accrual brought forward at 1 April 20X7	(2,070)
Commission income received during year	42,805
Income received post year end	1,960
Total commission income for the year	42,695

The commission income received during the year in the cash book of £42,805 is reduced by the amount which related to the prior year (the accrual of £2,070). The income received in the cash book in April 20X7 of £1,960 related to the year ended 31 March 20X7 therefore needs to be accrued at 31 March 20X7.

(e) **Which of the following can you use in your explanation to her?**

You must choose ONE answer for each row.

Reason for considering the receipt dated 15 April	Acceptable reason	Not acceptable reason
The proprietor of the business asked you to increase the profit for the year ended 31 March 20X7.		✓
The transaction is an expense relevant to the period ended 31 March 20X7.		✓
The figure is a current asset as at 31 March 20X7.	✓	

Explanation:

The figure is a genuine current asset (accrued income) as at 31 March 20X7. The asset is genuine (the cash has been fully received post year end) and the invoices confirm the service was supplied in the year ended 31 March 20X7, therefore it should be accrued at year end.

The transaction is income not expense.

It would be unethical for an accountant to make an adjustment to the financial statements to adjust profit for the proprietor to achieve a particular aim. Under the *AAT Code of Professional Ethics* should follow the principle of professional competence by preparing accounts in accordance with accounting standards rather than the proprietor's wishes.

Task 4 (23 marks)

(a) **Calculate the value of the adjustment required.**

£	– 46

Working:

The closing allowance for doubtful debts is calculated as 1% of the trade receivables (sales ledger control account) balance of £17,900 giving a figure of £179. There an opening allowance of £225, therefore a decrease of £46 (£225 – £179) is required.

(b) **(i)** Record this adjustment into the extract from the extended trial balance below.

(ii) Make the following further adjustments. You will NOT need to enter adjustments on every line. Do NOT enter zeros into unused cells.

Extract from the extended trial balance

Ledger account	Ledger balances		Adjustments	
	Dr £	Cr £	Dr £	Cr £
Allowance for doubtful debts		225	46	
Allowance for doubtful debts – adjustments				46
Bank	2,815			
Irrecoverable debts	390			
Office expenses	116,310			984
Plant at cost	25,400			900
Plant accumulated depreciation		12,250		
Prepaid expenses	505		450	
Purchases	108,265		984	
Purchases ledger control account		9,622		
Rent	14,800			
Sales		188,748		
Sales expenses	8,606			
Sales ledger control account	17,900			
Suspense		450	900	450

Working:

Purchases:

Should have done		Did do		Correction	
DR Purchases	984	DR Office expenses	984	DR Purchases	984
CR Cash	984	CR Cash	984	CR Office expenses	984

Prepayment:

Should have done	Did do	Correction
DR Prepaid expenses 450	DR Suspense 450	DR Prepaid expenses 450
CR Sales expenses 450	CR Sales expenses 450	CR Suspense 450

Plant:

This was posted to the trial balance as a debit of £25,400 instead of a debit of £24,500. This would have made the debits in the trial balance £900 (£25,400 – £24,500) higher than the credits, giving rise to a credit to the suspense account of £900 to make the TB balance. Therefore, the correction is:

DR Suspense   £900
CR Plant at cost   £900

(c) **Show the journal entries that will be required to close off the rent account for the financial year end and select an appropriate narrative.**

Journal

	Dr £	Cr £
Profit or loss account	14,800	
Rent		14,800

Narrative:

Transfer of rent for year ended 31 March 20X7 to the profit or loss account

(d) **What should you and your manager do next, and why? Choose ONE.**

	✓
Investigate the collectability of debts and delay completion of the accounts, as any adjustment could affect the outcome of the meeting.	✓
Investigate the collectability of debts and delay completion of the accounts because the client will have overstated the importance of the meeting.	
Complete the accounts by the deadline without any further adjustment, as any change is unlikely to be relevant to the meeting.	
Complete the accounts by the deadline without any further adjustment because the client's needs must take priority.	

Explanation:

It is important to ensure that all of the necessary work has been completed. By agreeing to complete the accounts at the insistence of the client, this is a threat to the fundamental principle of advocacy (whereby the client's position has been unduly promoted by the lack of work by the accountant) or even intimidation (undue pressure placed on them by the client). This goes against the *AAT Code of Professional Ethics*.

• •

Task 5 (20 marks)

(a) **Use the following table to show the THREE items that should appear on the cash book side of the reconciliation. Enter only ONE figure for each line. Do not enter zeros in unused cells.**

Adjustment	Dr £	Cr £
Adjustment 3		2,174
Adjustment 5		200
Adjustment 6		142

Explanation:

Adjustment 3 is the payment which needs to be reflected in the cashbook of £2,174. As the cash is leaving the bank account, it is a credit in the business' general ledger. Adjustment 5 is an understatement of the payment in the cashbook by £200 (£422 – £222), therefore a credit entry to decrease the cashbook balance is required. Adjustment 6 reflects the interest paid at the bank of £142, and therefore the cashbook balance needs to be reduced with a credit.

(b) **Which of the following statements about the net pay control account is TRUE? Choose ONE.**

The net pay control account…

	✓
…is a summary of memorandum accounts for each employee.	
…should have a balance of zero when all relevant entries have been correctly made.	✓
…will always be accurate when the bank reconciliation has been completed.	
…should include individual entries for gross pay due to each employee.	

(c) **Extend the figures into the statement of profit or loss and statement of financial position columns.**

Do NOT enter zeros into unused column cells.

Complete the extended trial balance by entering figures and a label in the correct places.

Extended trial balance

Ledger account	Ledger balances		Adjustments		Statement of profit or loss		Statement of financial position	
	Dr £	Cr £	Dr £	Cr £	Dr £	Cr £	Dr £	Cr £
Bank		958		75				1,033
Capital		11,000						11,000
Closing inventory			9,930	9,930		9,930	9,930	
Depreciation charges	3,895				3,895			
Equipment at cost	20,162			689			19,473	
Equipment accumulated depreciation		15,579						15,579
Interest paid	63		75		138			
Loan		6,566	1,085					5,481
Office expenses	22,495		689	290	22,894			
Opening inventory	10,058				10,058			
Payroll expenses	20,825				20,825			
Prepayments			290				290	
Purchases	79,454				79,454			
Purchases ledger control account		13,167						13,167
Sales		126,139		485		126,624		
Sales ledger control account	16,979						16,979	
Suspense	600		485	1,085				
VAT		1,122						1,122
Profit/loss for the year						710	710	
Total	174,531	174,531	12,554	12,554	**137,264**	**137,264**	**47,382**	**47,382**

AAT AQ2016 SAMPLE ASSESSMENT 2 ADVANCED BOOKKEEPING

You are advised to attempt sample assessment 2 online from the AAT website. This will ensure you are prepared for how the assessment will be presented on the AAT's system when you attempt the real assessment. Please access the assessment using the address below:

https://www.aat.org.uk/training/study-support/search

The AAT may call the assessments on their website, under study support resources, either a 'practice assessment' or 'sample assessment'.

AAT AQ2016 SAMPLE ASSESSMENT 2

BPP PRACTICE ASSESSMENT 1
ADVANCED BOOKKEEPING

Time allowed: 2 hours

Advanced Bookkeeping (AVBK)
BPP practice assessment 1

Task 1

This task is about non-current assets.

You are working on the accounting records of a business known as RTL Trading.

You may ignore VAT in this task.

The following is an extract from a purchase invoice received by RTL Trading:

Fittings Supplies plc Unit 76 East Trading Estate Mendlesham ME2 9FG	Invoice 9032	Date:	20 June 20X5
To:	RTL Trading 14 Larkmead Road Mendlesham ME6 2PO		
Description	Item number	Quantity	£
Warehouse racking system	WR617	1	2,000.00
Delivery and set-up charges		1	200.00
Specialist oil for racking @ £15.00 per litre		3 litres	45.00
Net total			2,245.00

The acquisition has been made under a hire purchase agreement.

The following information relates to the sale of an item of machinery:

Identification number	MC5267
Date of sale	22 June 20X5
Selling price	£3,250.00

- RTL Trading has a policy of capitalising expenditure over £200.

- Furniture and fittings are depreciated at 25% using the straight line method. There are no residual values.

- Machinery is depreciated at 40% using the diminishing balance method.
- A full year's depreciation is charged in the year of acquisition and none in the year of sale.

(a) For the year ended 30 September 20X5, record the following in the non-current assets register below:
- **Any acquisitions of non-current assets**
- **Any disposals of non-current assets**
- **Depreciation**

Extract from non-current assets register

Description	Acquisition date	Cost £	Depreciation charges £	Carrying amount £	Funding method	Disposal proceeds £	Disposal date
Furniture and fittings							
Racking system WR290	01/12/X2	6,000.00			Loan		
Year end 30/09/X3			1,500.00	4,500.00			
Year end 30/09/X4			1,500.00	3,000.00			
Year end 30/09/X5							
▼1	▼2					▼3	
Year end 30/09/X5							
Machinery							
Machine MC5267	01/10/X2	7,500.00			Cash		
Year end 30/09/X3			3,000.00	4,500.00			
Year end 30/09/X4			1,800.00	2,700.00			
Year end 30/09/X5			▼4	▼5			▼2
Machine MC5298	31/01/X4	8,800.00			Part exchange		
Year end 30/09/X4			3,520.00	5,280.00			
Year end 30/09/X5							

Picklist 1:

Machine MC5267
Machine MC5298
Racking system WR290
Racking system WR617

Picklist 2:

01/12/X2
01/10/X2
31/01/X4
20/06/X5
22/06/X5

Picklist 3:

Cash
Finance lease
Hire purchase
Loan

Picklist 4:

0.00
810.00
1,080.00
1,875.00

Picklist 5:

0.00
825.00
1,620.00
1,890.00

RTL Trading is planning its non-current asset purchases for the next year. The business currently has a large bank overdraft and very high borrowings. All existing bank loans are secured on non-current assets and no further assets are available to offer as security. All non-current assets are currently in working order and needed for the business. The business wishes to become the legal owner of the asset.

(b) **Which one of the following would be the most suitable funding method for the next purchase of non-current assets?**

	✓
Cash	
Bank loan	
Hire purchase	
Finance lease	

Task 2

This task is about accounting for non-current assets.

- You are working on the accounting records of a business for the year ended 31 December 20X7. The business is registered for VAT.

- On 1 September 20X7 the business bought a new machine for the business.

- The machine cost £14,640 including VAT; this was paid from the bank.

- The machine's residual value is expected to be £2,300, excluding VAT.

- The business's depreciation policy for machines is 10% per annum on a straight line basis. A full year's depreciation is charged in the year of acquisition and none in the year of disposal.

- Depreciation has already been entered into the accounts for the business's existing machines.

(a) **Calculate the depreciation charge for the year on the new machine.**

£

Make entries to account for:

- **The acquisition of the new machine**
- **The depreciation on the new machine**

On each account, show clearly the balance carried down or transferred to the statement of profit or loss.

Machines at cost

	£		£
Balance b/d	20,000	 ▼	
▼		▼	

Depreciation charges

	£		£
Balance b/d	5,700	▼	
▼		▼	

Machines accumulated depreciation

	£		£
▼		Balance b/d	8,600
▼		▼	

VAT control account

	£		£
▼		Balance b/d	4,200
▼		▼	

Picklist:

Balance b/d
Balance c/d
Bank
Depreciation charges
Disposals
Machines accumulated depreciation
Machines at cost
Machines running expenses
Profit or loss account
Purchases

Purchases ledger control account
Sales
Sales ledger control account
VAT control account

The business sold a vehicle which originally cost £15,000, net of VAT. At the date of disposal, accumulated depreciation amounted to £10,000. The selling price of the vehicle was £7,500, net of VAT.

(b) **What is the gain or loss on disposal?**

	Amount £
▼	

Picklist:

Gain
Loss

(c) **Show the journal entry required to remove the accumulated depreciation of the vehicle from the general ledger.**

	Amount £	Debit ✓	Credit ✓
▼			
▼			

Picklist:

Bank
Depreciation charges
Disposals
Machines accumulated depreciation
Machines at cost
Machines running expenses
Profit or loss account
Purchases
Purchases ledger control account
Sales
Sales ledger control account
Vehicles accumulated depreciation
Vehicles at cost
VAT control account

Task 3

This task is about ledger accounting, including accruals and prepayments, and applying ethical principles.

(a) **Enter the figures given in the table below in the appropriate trial balance columns.**

Do not enter zeros in unused column cells.

Do not enter any figures as negatives.

Extract from trial balance as at 30 June 20X4

Account	Ledger balance £	Trial balance Debit £	Credit £
Capital	10,000		
Discounts received	1,209		
Interest expense	201		
Irrecoverable debts	780		

You are working on the final accounts of a business for the year ended 30 June 20X4. In this task, you can ignore VAT.

Business policy: accounting for accruals and prepayments

An entry is made into the income or expense account and an opposite entry into the relevant asset or liability account. In the following period, this entry is removed.

You are now looking at rental income for the year. There was a prepayment of rental income at 30 June 20X3.

The cash book for the year shows receipts of rental income of £5,000. Included in this figure is £270 for the quarter ended 31 July 20X4.

(b) **Calculate the value of the adjustment required for rental income as at 30 June 20X4.**

Enter an increase to rental income as a positive number and a decrease as a negative number.

£

Update the rental income account. Show clearly:

- **The cash book figure**
- **The year end adjustment**
- **The transfer to the statement of profit or loss for the year**

Rental income

	£		£
▼		Prepaid income (reversal)	250
▼		▼	
▼		▼	

Picklist:

Accrued income
Accrued income (reversal)
Balance c/d
Bank
Capital
Discounts received
Irrecoverable debts
Interest expense
Prepaid income
Prepaid income (reversal)
Profit or loss account
Statement of financial position

You are now looking at selling expense for the year.

Selling expenses of £87 were accrued on 30 June 20X3.

(c) Complete the following statements:

The reversal of the accrual is dated [▼].

The reversal is on the [▼] side of the selling expenses account.

Picklist:

30 June 20X3
1 July 20X3
1 July 20X4

credit
debit

The cash book for the year shows payments for selling expenses of £2,850.

In July 20X4, an invoice for £63 was received for costs incurred in June 20X4.

(d) Taking into account all the information you have, calculate the selling expenses for the year ended 30 June 20X4.

£ [   ]

A trainee colleague asks you why you are making adjustments for accruals and prepayments at the year end.

(e) Which of the following can you use in your explanation to her?

You must choose ONE answer for each row.

Reason for considering accruals and prepayments	Acceptable reason ✓	Not acceptable reason ✓
Adjustments are a way of manipulating profits to give a favourable impression of the business.		
Income and expenditure must be matched to the accounting period to which they relate.		
The timing of receipts and payments does not always align with the business's accounting periods.		

Task 4

This task is about accounting adjustments.

You are a trainee accountant reporting to a managing partner in an accounting practice. You are working on the accounting records of a business client.

A trial balance has been drawn up and balanced using a suspense account. You now need to make some corrections and adjustments for the year ended 31 December 20X4.

You may ignore VAT in this task.

Closing inventory has been recorded in the trial balance. However, one item of inventory which has been included at its cost of £750 has a selling price of £680 and a further £90 must be spent to complete the inventory before it can be sold. Selling costs are expected to amount to 5% of the selling price.

(a) Calculate the value of the adjustment required to closing inventory.

Enter an increase to inventory as a positive number and a decrease to inventory as a negative number.

£	

(b) **(i)** Record this adjustment into the extract from the extended trial balance below.

(ii) Make the following further adjustments.

You will NOT need to enter adjustments on every line. Do NOT enter zeros into unused cells.

- The allowance for doubtful debts needs to be adjusted to 3% of the outstanding trade receivables.

- Discounts received of £257 have only been entered into the purchases ledger control account from the discounts received day book.

- The office expenses account in the general ledger correctly shows a balance of £38,430. This has been incorrectly transferred to the trial balance as £34,830.

Extract from the extended trial balance

Ledger account	Ledger balances		Adjustments	
	Debit £	Credit £	Debit £	Credit £
Allowance for doubtful debts		900		
Allowance for doubtful debts – adjustments				
Bank	8,445			
Closing inventory – statement of financial position	22,600			
Closing inventory – statement of profit or loss		22,600		
Discounts received				
Irrecoverable debts	1,170			
Office expenses	34,830			
Plant accumulated depreciation		36,750		
Plant at cost	76,200			
Prepaid expenses	1,515			
Purchases	324,795			
Purchases ledger control account		28,866		
Sales		566,244		
Sales expenses	25,818			
Sales ledger control account	53,700			
Suspense	3,343			

(c) **Show the journal entries that will be required to close off the sales account for the financial year end and select an appropriate narrative.**

Journal

	Debit £	Credit £
▼		
▼		

Narrative:

	▼

Picklist:

Allowance for doubtful debts
Allowance for doubtful debts – adjustment
Bank
Closing inventory – statement of financial position
Closing inventory – statement of profit or loss
Discounts received
Irrecoverable debts
Office expenses
Plant accumulated depreciation
Plant at cost
Prepaid expenses
Profit of loss account
Purchases ledger control account
Rent
Sales
Sales expenses
Sales ledger control account
Statement of financial position
Suspense

Closure of general ledger for the year ended 31 December 20X4
Closure of sales account to the suspense account
Transfer of sales for year ended 31 December 20X4 to the profit or loss account
Transfer of sales for year ended 31 December 20X4 to the statement of financial position

Your manager has now reviewed the resulting figures in the draft accounts. He is concerned that the client may have significantly overstated the profit for the year ended 31 December 20X4 as it is much higher than both the budgeted and prior year figures. You are aware that the client is trying to persuade his friend to invest in the business and that he has already passed the draft accounts on to his friend to review.

(d) What should you and your manager do next, and why? Choose ONE.

	✓
Take no action because if the profit figure is amended, the client could lose out on the investment from his friend	
Take no action because the client is a longstanding one and the fee our firm earns from him is substantial	
Request a meeting with the client to discuss why the profit is higher than budget and prior year to try and ascertain whether it is due to genuine business transactions	
Email the client's friend to warn him not to invest because the profit might be overstated	

Task 5

This task is about period end routines, using accounting records and the extended trial balance.

You are preparing the sales ledger control account reconciliation for a sole trader.

The balance showing on the sales ledger control account is £5,097 and the total of the list of sales ledger balances is £4,144.

The sales ledger control account has been compared with the total of the list of balances from the sales ledger and the following points noted.

1. The sales ledger column in the cash book – debit side was undercast by £100.

2. A contra for £76 was only recorded in the sales ledger.

3. An invoice for £536 in the sales day book was not posted to the sales ledger.

4. A total in the sales returns day book of £489 was recorded in the general ledger as £498.

5. A balance of £250 was omitted for the sales ledger listing.

6. A cash receipt of £95 from A Smith was accidentally posted to the sales ledger account of J Smith.

(a) **Use the following table to show the THREE adjustments you need to make to the sales ledger control account.**

Adjustment	Amount £	Debit ✓	Credit ✓
▼			
▼			
▼			

Picklist:

Adjustment 1
Adjustment 2
Adjustment 3
Adjustment 4
Adjustment 5
Adjustment 6

(b) **Which of the following statements about bank reconciliations are TRUE?**

Select ONE answer for each row.

	True ✓	False ✓
A bank reconciliation helps identify items missing from the cash book		
A bank reconciliation forms part of the general ledger		
The balance on the bank statement is the balance that should be posted to the trial balance		
Items in the cash book but not in the bank statement may relate to timing differences		

(c) **Extend the figures into the statement of profit or loss and statement of financial position columns.**

Do NOT enter zeros into unused column cells.

Make the columns balance by entering figures and a label in the correct places.

Extended trial balance

Ledger account	Ledger balances		Adjustments		Statement of profit or loss		Statement of financial position	
	Dr £	Cr £	Dr £	Cr £	Dr £	Cr £	Dr £	Cr £
Administration expenses	6,739			569				
Allowance for doubtful debts		1,347		203				
Allowance for doubtful debts adjustment			203					
Bank		5,290						
Capital		9,460						
Closing inventory			7,234	7,234				
Depreciation charges			7,800					
Machinery accumulated depreciation		62,400		7,800				
Machinery at cost	115,000		750					
Marketing	7,365							
Opening inventory	9,933							
Purchases	34,289							
Purchases ledger control account		5,096						
Sales		112,015		3,000				
Sales ledger control account	8,023							
Suspense		8,819	9,569	750				
VAT		6,300						
Wages and salaries	29,378			6,000				
▼								
	210,727	210,727	25,556	25,556				

BPP
LEARNING MEDIA

Picklist:

Balance b/d
Balance c/d
Gross profit/loss for the year
Profit/loss for the year
Suspense

BPP PRACTICE ASSESSMENT 1
ADVANCED BOOKKEEPING

ANSWERS

Advanced Bookkeeping (AVBK)
BPP practice assessment 1

Task 1

(a) Non-current assets register

Description	Acquisition date	Cost £	Depreciation charges £	Carrying amount £	Funding method	Disposal proceeds £	Disposal date
Furniture and fittings							
Racking system WR290	01/12/X2	6,000.00			Loan		
Year end 30/09/X3			1,500.00	4,500.00			
Year end 30/09/X4			1,500.00	3,000.00			
Year end 30/09/X5			**1,500.00**	**1,500.00**			
Racking system WR617	**20/06/X5**	**2,200.00**			**Hire purchase**		
Year end 30/09/X5			**550.00**	**1,650.00**			
Machinery							
Machine MC5267	01/10/X2	7,500.00			Cash		
Year end 30/09/X3			3,000.00	4,500.00			
Year end 30/09/X4			1,800.00	2,700.00			
Year end 30/09/X5			**0.00**	**0.00**		3,250.00	22/06/X5
Machine MC5298	31/01/X4	8,800.00			Part exchange		
Year end 30/09/X4			3,520.00	5,280.00			
Year end 30/09/X5			**2,112.00**	**3,168.00**			

Explanations:

For the new racking system (WR617), the purchase price (£2,000.00) and directly attributable costs (£200.00 delivery and set up) are capitalised but the specialist oil is revenue expenditure and as such, should be expensed in profit or loss which is why it is not recorded in the non-current asset register. Depreciation is calculated at 25% of cost using the straight line basis and is not pro-rated as the policy is to charge a full year in the year of acquisition: £2,200.00 × 25% = £550.00.

For machine MC5267 which is sold in the year, no depreciation should be charged as the accounting policy is a full year in the year of acquisition and none in the year of sale. The carrying amount is cleared to zero as the asset has been sold.

For machine MC5298, as the depreciation is charged at 40% using the diminishing balance method, depreciation is calculated as £5,280.00 × 40% = £2,112.00.

(b)

	✓
Cash	
Bank loan	
Hire purchase	✓
Finance lease	

Explanation:

Cash is not appropriate as the business currently has a large overdraft. Nor is a bank loan suitable as the business currently has very high borrowings so a bank is unlikely to lend particularly as no non-current assets are available to offer as security. Of the remaining two options, hire purchase is more suitable as under a hire purchase agreement, the business always becomes the legal owner of the asset which is not necessarily the case with a finance lease.

Task 2

(a)

£	990

Working:

As the business is VAT registered, it can recover the VAT on the new machine from HMRC. Therefore, the cost to the business is the amount excluding VAT which is calculated as £14,640 × 100/120 = £12,200. When the business sells the machine, VAT on the sales price will be payable to HMRC, therefore, the residual value excludes VAT when calculating depreciation.

VAT on the new machine is: £12,200 × 20% = £2,440.

Depreciation = (£12,200 – £2,300) × 10% = £990

Machines at cost

	£		£
Balance b/d	20,000	**Balance c/d**	**32,200**
Bank	**12,200**		
	32,200		**32,200**

Depreciation charges

	£		£
Balance b/d	5,700	**Profit or loss account**	**6,690**
Machines accumulated depreciation	**990**		
	6,690		**6,690**

Machines accumulated depreciation

	£		£
Balance c/d	**9,590**	Balance b/d	8,600
		Depreciation charges	**990**
	9,590		**9,590**

VAT control account

	£		£
Bank	2,440	Balance b/d	4,200
Balance c/d	1,760		
	4,200		4,200

(b)   Gain or loss on disposal

	Amount £
Gain	2,500

Working:

	£
Sales proceeds (net of VAT)	7,500
Carrying amount (£15,000 – £10,000)	(5,000)
Gain	2,500

Note. When calculating the gain or loss on disposal, VAT is excluded from the sales price as it is payable to HMRC and it is also excluded from the purchase price as that VAT would have been reclaimed from the HMRC. This is because the business is VAT registered.

(c)   Journal entry

	Amount £	Debit ✓	Credit ✓
Vehicles accumulated depreciation	10,000	✓	
Disposals	10,000		✓

Task 3

(a) Extract from trial balance as at 30 June 20X4

Account	Ledger balance £	Trial balance Debit £	Trial balance Credit £
Capital	10,000		10,000
Discounts received	1,209		1,209
Interest expense	201	201	
Irrecoverable debts	780	780	

(b)

£	– 90

Working:

Prepaid income = 1/3 × £270 = £90

This needs to be removed from income as it relates to next year (July 20X4).

Rental income

	£		£
Prepaid income	90	Prepaid income (reversal)	250
Profit and loss account	5,160	Bank	5,000
	5,250		**5,250**

(c)

The reversal of the accrual is dated   1 July 20X3 .

The reversal is on the   credit   side of the selling expenses account.

(d)

£	2,826

Working:

The expense for the year is calculated as:

£2,850 cash paid – £87 paid in relation to prior year + £63 owing at the year end

Alternatively you can use a ledger account to help you work out your answer.

Selling expenses

	£		£
Bank	2,850	Accrued expenses (reversal)	87
Accrual	63	Profit or loss account	2,826
	2,913		2,913

(e) Explanation:

Reason for considering accruals and prepayments	Acceptable reason ✓	Not acceptable reason ✓
Adjustments are a way of manipulating profits to give a favourable impression of the business.		✓
Income and expenditure must be matched to the accounting period to which they relate.	✓	
The timing of receipts and payments does not always align with the business's accounting periods.	✓	

Task 4

(a)

£	– 194

Working:

Inventory should be valued at the lower of its cost of £750 and net realisable value of £556 (£680 – £90 – [5% × £680]). Therefore, a write down of £194 (£750 – £556) is required:

DR Closing inventory – statement of profit or loss £194
CR Closing inventory – statement of financial position £194

(b) Extract from the extended trial balance

Ledger account	Ledger balances		Adjustments	
	Debit £	Credit £	Debit £	Credit £
Allowance for doubtful debts		900		**711**
Allowance for doubtful debts – adjustments			**711**	
Bank	8,445			
Closing inventory – statement of financial position	22,600			**194**
Closing inventory – statement of profit or loss		22,600	**194**	
Discounts received				**257**
Irrecoverable debts	1,170			
Office expenses	34,830		**3,600**	
Plant accumulated depreciation		36,750		
Plant at cost	76,200			
Prepaid expenses	1,515			
Purchases	324,795			
Purchases ledger control account		28,866		
Sales		566,244		
Sales expenses	25,818			
Sales ledger control account	53,700			
Suspense	3,343		**257**	**3,600**

Explanation:

Allowance for doubtful debts

This needs to be increased to 3% of the outstanding trade receivables (sales ledger control account) balance of £53,700. This comes to £1,611. The current allowance per the TB is £900, so an increase of £711 (£1,611 - £900) is required.

DR Allowance for doubtful debts – adjustments   £711
CR Allowance for doubtful debts   £711

Discounts received

Should have done	Did do	Correction
DR PLCA £257	DR PLCA £257	DR Suspense £257
CR Discounts received £257	CR Suspense £257	CR Discounts received £257

Office expenses

The balance in the TB needs to be increased from £34,830 to £38,430 – resulting in an increase of £3,600. As the balance was initially incorrectly listed in the TB as too small a debit balance (as expenses are a debit balance), it would have resulted in an imbalance and the need for a debit to suspense to make the TB balance. Therefore, the correcting entry is:

DR Office expenses   £3,600
CR Suspense   £3,600

(c)   Journal

	Debit £	Credit £
Sales	566,244	
Profit and loss account		566,244

Narrative:

Transfer of sales for year ended 31 December 20X4 to the profit or loss account

(d)

	✓
Take no action because if the profit figure is amended, the client could lose out on the investment from his friend	
Take no action because the client is a longstanding one and the fee our firm earns from him is substantial	
Request a meeting with the client to discuss why the profit is higher than budget and prior year to try and ascertain whether it is due to genuine business transactions	✓
Email the client's friend to warn him not to invest because the profit might be overstated	

Explanation:

As an AAT accounting technician, you are bound by the AAT's Code of Professional Ethics and to comply with the fundamental principle of professional competence and due care, you need to respond appropriately to period end pressures and ensure that the accounts do not contain misleading or inaccurate information. Therefore, taking no action is not an option. Emailing the client's friend would be a breach of the fundamental principle of confidentiality so is not an acceptable option. The correct action to take here is to try and understand why the profit is higher than expected by having a direct discussion with the client because there might be genuine business reasons.

Task 5

(a)

Adjustment	Amount £	Debit ✓	Credit ✓
Adjustment for 1	100		✓
Adjustment for 2	76		✓
Adjustment for 4	9	✓	

Explanation:

Adjustments 3 and 5 only affect the total of the list of sales ledger accounts. Although adjustment 6 affects the individual sales ledger accounts of A Smith and J Smith, it will not affect the total of the list of balances.

(b)

	True ✓	False ✓
A bank reconciliation helps identify items missing from the cash book	✓	
A bank reconciliation forms part of the general ledger		✓
The balance on the bank statement is the balance that should be posted to the trial balance		✓
Items in the cash book but not in the bank statement may relate to timing differences	✓	

(c)

Ledger account	Ledger balances		Adjustments		Statement of profit or loss		Statement of financial position	
	Dr £	Cr £	Dr £	Cr £	Dr £	Cr £	Dr £	Cr £
Administration expenses	6,739			569	**6,170**			
Allowance for doubtful debts		1,347		203				**1,550**
Allowance for doubtful debts – adjustment			203		**203**			
Bank		5,290						**5,290**
Capital		9,460						**9,460**
Closing inventory			7,234	7,234		**7,234**	**7,234**	
Depreciation charges			7,800		**7,800**			
Machinery accumulated depreciation		62,400		7,800				**70,200**
Machinery at cost	115,000		750				**115,750**	
Marketing	7,365				**7,365**			
Opening inventory	9,933				**9,933**			
Purchases	34,289				**34,289**			
Purchases ledger control account		5,096						**5,096**
Sales		112,015		3,000		**115,015**		
Sales ledger control account	8,023						**8,023**	
Suspense		8,819	9,569	750				
VAT		6,300						**6,300**
Wages and salaries	29,378			6,000	**23,378**			
Profit/loss for the year					**33,111**			**33,111**
	210,727	210,727	25,556	25,556	**122,249**	**122,249**	**131,007**	**131,007**

BPP PRACTICE ASSESSMENT 2
ADVANCED BOOKKEEPING

Time allowed: 2 hours

BPP PRACTICE ASSESSMENT 2
ADVANCED BOOKKEEPING

Time allowed: 2 hours

Advanced Bookkeeping (AVBK)
BPP practice assessment 2

Task 1

This task is about non-current assets.

You are working on the accounting records of a business known as Hagbourne.

Hagbourne is registered for VAT and its year end is 31 March.

The business has part exchanged an item of machinery used in its workshop.

The following is the relevant purchase invoice:

Office Supplies Ltd 28 High Street Cridley CR4 6AS	Invoice 198233	Date:	1 December 20X5
To:	Hagbourne & Co 67 Foggarty Street Cridley CR9 0TT		
Description	**Item number**	**Quantity**	**£**
Modular office workstation system	OFF783	1	6,500.00
Delivery and assembly charges		1	295.00
Printer paper		75 reams	200.00
Net			6,995.00
VAT @ 20%			1,399.00
Total			8,394.00
Part exchange with workstation GT551. Balance £6,048 settled by hire purchase agreement.			

VAT can be reclaimed on the purchase of these items.

The following information relates to the workstation replaced:

Identification number	GT551
Date of purchase	1 July 20X3
Date of sale	1 December 20X5
Part exchange value	£1955.00 + VAT

- Hagbourne's policy is to recognise items of capital expenditure over £100 as non-current assets.

- Office equipment is depreciated over a useful life of five years on a straight line basis. A residual value of 25% of cost is assumed.

- Motor vehicles are depreciated at 40% per annum using the diminishing balance method.

- Depreciation is calculated on an annual basis and charged in equal instalments for each full month an asset is owned.

(a) For the year ended 31 March 20X6, record the following in extract from the non-current assets register below:

- **Any acquisitions of non-current assets**
- **Any disposals of non-current assets**
- **Depreciation**

Show your numerical answers to TWO decimal places.

Use the DD/MM/YY format for any dates.

Note. **Not every cell will require an entry, and not all cells will accept entries.**

Extract from Non-current assets register

Description	Acquisition date	Cost £	Depreciation charges £	Carrying amount £	Funding method	Disposal proceeds £	Disposal date
Motor vehicles							
Car CR04 YTR	01/04/X3	18,000.00			Cash		
Year end 31/03/X4			7,200.00	10,800.00			
Year end 31/03/X5			4,320.00	6,480.00			
Year end 31/03/X6							
Office equipment							
Desk OFF253	01/01/X4	10,000.00			Finance lease		
Year end 31/03/X4			375.00	9,625.00			
Year end 31/03/X5			1,500.00	8,125.00			
Year end 31/03/X6							
▼ (1)	▼ (2)				▼ (3)		
Year end 31/03/X6							
Workstation GT551	01/07/X3	5,210.00			Cash		
Year end 31/03/X4			586.00	4,624.00			
Year end 31/03/X4			782.00	3,842.00			
Year end 31/03/X4			▼ (4)	▼ (5)			▼ (6)

(1) Picklist for description:

Car CR04 YTR
Desk OFF253
Workstation GT551
Workstation OFF783

(2) Picklist for acquisition date:

01/07/X3
01/04/X5
01/12/X5
31/03/X6

(3) Picklist for funding method:

Cash
Finance lease
Hire purchase
Loan

(4) Picklist for depreciation charges:

0.00
391.00
586.00
782.00

(5) Picklist for carrying amount:

0.00
3,060.00
3,256.00
3,842.00

(6) Picklist for disposal date:

01/07/X3
01/04/X5
01/12/X5
31/03/X6

(b) **Which ONE of the following best describes the residual value of a non-current asset?**

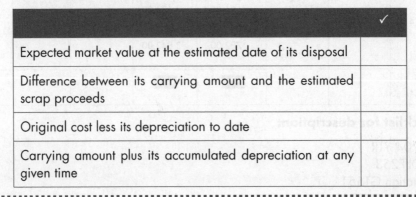

	✓
Expected market value at the estimated date of its disposal	
Difference between its carrying amount and the estimated scrap proceeds	
Original cost less its depreciation to date	
Carrying amount plus its accumulated depreciation at any given time	

Task 2

This task is about ledger accounting for non-current assets.

- You are working on the accounts of a business which is not registered for VAT. The business's year end is 31 December 20X6.

- An item of machinery was part exchanged for a newer model on 1 January 20X6.

- The original machinery cost £2,000 on 1 January 20X3.

- The business's depreciation policy for machinery is 20% using the diminishing balance method.

- A full year's depreciation is applied in the year of acquisition and none in the year of disposal.

- A part exchange allowance of £350 was given.

- £950 was paid from the bank to complete the purchase.

(a) **Complete the following tasks relating to the original machinery:**

(i) **Calculate the accumulated depreciation at 31 December 20X5.**

£	

(ii) **Complete the disposals account. Show clearly the balance to be carried down or transferred to the statement of profit or loss, as appropriate.**

Disposals

	£		£
▾		▾	
▾		▾	
▾		▾	

Picklist:

Bank
Machinery accumulated depreciation
Machinery at cost
Profit or loss account

(b) **Complete the tasks below:**

(i) **Calculate the purchase cost of the new machinery from the information above.**

£ [   ]

Before the part-exchange entries were posted, the balance on the machinery at cost account was £18,050.

The entries have now been correctly made.

(ii) **Complete the sentence:**

The machinery at cost account will have a final balance carried down

of £ [   ] when the ledger accounts are closed

for the year.

On 1 November 20X6, new fixtures and fittings were purchased. These were bought with a loan from the bank. You are given the following information:

* Purhase cost: £1,985
* Depreciation charged for the year ended 31/12/X6: £97

(c) **Complete the journal below.**

Account	Amount £	Debit ✓	Credit ✓
▼			
▼			
Narrative:			
Depreciation charged for the year ended 31 December 20X6 for fixtures and fittings purchased 1 November 20X6			

Picklist:

Depreciation charges
Bank
Fixture and fittings accumulated depreciation

Task 3

This task is about ledger accounting, including accruals and prepayments.

You are working on the final accounts of a business for the year ended 30 September 20X6. In this task, you can ignore VAT.

Business policy: accounting for accruals and prepayments

An entry is made into the income or expense account and an opposite entry into the relevant asset or liability account. In the following period, this entry is removed.

You are looking at commission income:

The cash book for the year shows receipts of commission income of £496. Commission of £63 is still due for September 20X6 at the year end.

(a) Update the rental income account. Show clearly:

- **The cash book figure**
- **The year end adjustment**
- **The transfer to the statement of profit or loss for the year**

Commission income

	£		£
Accrued income (reversal)	175	▼	
▼		▼	

Picklist:

Accrued expenses
Accrued income
Balance b/d
Balance c/d
Bank
Commission income
Prepaid expenses
Prepaid income
Profit or loss account
Sales
Sales ledger control account

(b) **Answer the following regarding the accrued income reversal of £175 in the commission income account above.**

(i) **How were the elements of the accounting equation affected by this transaction?**

Tick ONE box for each row.

	Increase ✓	Decrease ✓	No change ✓
Assets			
Liabilities			
Equity			

(ii) **Which ONE of the following dates should be entered for this transaction in the ledger account? Tick the appropriate box.**

	✓
1 October 20X5	
30 September 20X5	
30 September 20X6	

You are now looking at stationary expenses for the year.

There is an opening prepayment of £134 for the year ended 30 September 20X6.

The cash book for the year shows payments for stationery of £798. In September 20X6, £48 was paid for items delivered and used in October 20X6.

(c) **Complete the following statement:**

The stationery expenses account needs an adjustment for

[　　　　　▼] of £ [　　　　　　] dated [　　　　▼] .

Picklist:

Description:
Accrued expenses
Prepaid expenses
Amount:
£798
£48
Date:
30 September 20X6
1 October 20X7

(d) **Taking into account all the information you have, calculate the stationary expense for the year ended 30 September 20X6.**

£	

....

Task 4

This task is about accounting adjustments.

You are working as an accounting technician for a sole trader business with a year end of 31 December. A trial balance has been drawn up and a suspense account opened with a credit balance of £1,826. You now need to make some corrections and adjustments for the year ended 31 December 20X6.

You may ignore VAT for this task.

Record the journal entries needed in the general ledger to deal with the items below.

You should:

- **Remove any incorrect entries where appropriate**
- **Post the correct entries**

Do NOT enter zeros into unused column cells.

Note. You do NOT need to give narratives.

(a) **No entries have been made for an irrecoverable debt of £672.**

Account		Debit £	Credit £
	▼		
	▼		

Picklist:

Allowance for doubtful debts
Allowance for doubtful debts – adjustments
Irrecoverable debts
Profit or loss account
Sales ledger control account
Suspense

(b) Drawings of £850 have been made. The correct entry was made in the cash book but no other entries were made.

Account		Debit £	Credit £
▼			
▼			

Picklist:

Drawings
Bank
Suspense account

(c) Closing inventory for the year end 31 December 20X6 has not yet been recorded. Its value at cost is £9,350. Included in this figure are some items costing £345 that will be sold for £200.

Account		Debit £	Credit £
▼			
▼			

Picklist:

Closing inventory – statement of financial position
Closing inventory – statement of profit or loss

(d) Credit notes of £1,338 have been posted to the correct side of the purchases ledger control account, but have been made to the same side of the purchases returns account.

Account		Debit £	Credit £
▼			
▼			

Picklist:

Purchase ledger control account
Sales ledger control account
Purchase returns
Suspense
Sales returns

Now that you have posted the journals, you are pleased to see that the suspense account is clear and the trial balance totals agree.

(e) **Complete the following sentence:**

▼

conclude that the balances included are now free from all errors.

▼

conclude that the inventory valuation as at 31 December 20X6 is included in the trial balance.

Picklist:

I can
I cannot

(f) **Which ONE of the these would be acceptable professional behaviour if actioned by you?**

	✓
A client's sales manager wants you to accrue for a bonus based on the current year sales. The bank statement shows that the bonus was paid in the next financial year.	
A client wants to improve his profit figure. She asks you to delay recording a liability until after the year end.	
One of the client's credit customers is going out of business. You feel this news can be disregarded as the effective date of the business closure is after the year end date.	
Your firm needs to meet its deadline for preparing the final accounts. Your supervisor tells you to save time by using net realisable value for all items in the inventory valuation.	

Task 5

This task is about period end routines, using accounting records and the extended trial balance.

You are preparing a purchase ledger control account reconciliation for a sole trader.

The balance showing on the purchases ledger control account is £7,092 and the total of the list of purchases ledger balances is £3,309.

The purchase ledger control account and the purchase ledger have been compared and the following items noted:

1. Total discounts received of £1,489 were only recorded in the discounts received account.

2. A purchases ledger column of £1,267 in the cash book – credit side was not posted to the purchases ledger control account.

3. A contra for £123 was recorded in the purchases ledger control account but not in the individual supplier account.

4. The total column in the purchases returns day book was overcast by £180.

5. A supplier account with a credit balance of £580 was omitted from the total.

6. A purchase invoice of £375 was posted to the supplier account as a credit note.

(a) **Use the following table to show the THREE adjustments you need to make to the purchases ledger control account.**

Adjustment	Amount £	Debit ✓	Credit ✓
▼			
▼			
▼			

Picklist:

Adjustment 1
Adjustment 2
Adjustment 3
Adjustment 4
Adjustment 5
Adjustment 6

(b) **To reduce the allowance for doubtful debts we must:**

Choose ONE.

	✓
Credit the allowance for doubtful debts account	
Debit the irrecoverable debts account	
Credit the allowance for doubtful debts adjustment account	
Credit the sales ledger control account	
None of the above	

You are now working on the accounting records of a different business.

You have the following extended trial balance. The adjustments have already been correctly entered.

(c) **Extend the figures into the statement of profit or loss and statement of financial position columns.**

Do NOT enter zeros into unused column cells.

Make the columns balance by entering figures and a label in the correct places.

Extended trial balance

Ledger account	Ledger balances Dr £	Cr £	Adjustments Dr £	Cr £	Statement of profit or loss Dr £	Cr £	Statement of financial position Dr £	Cr £
Bank	5,246							
Capital		19,600						
Closing inventory			6,712	6,712				
Depreciation charges	4,298		4,000					
Discounts received		2,291		1,325				
Drawings	11,712		9,826					
Irrecoverable debts	627							
Motor expenses	2,065							
Motor vehicles accumulated depreciation		12,500		4,000				
Motor vehicles at cost	20,000							
Office expenses	7,219							
Opening inventory	4,820							
Purchases	91,289							
Purchases ledger control account		7,109	786					
Salaries	32,781		3,484					
Sales		156,782						
Sales ledger control account	11,092							
Suspense	12,771		1,325	14,096				
VAT		5,638						
▼								
	203,920	203,920	26,133	26,133				

Picklist:

Balance b/d
Balance c/d
Gross profit/loss for the year
Profit/loss for the year
Suspense

BPP PRACTICE ASSESSMENT 2 ADVANCED BOOKKEEPING

ANSWERS

Advanced Bookkeeping (AVBK)
BPP practice assessment 2

Task 1

(a) Non-current assets register

Description	Acquisition date	Cost £	Depreciation charges £	Carrying amount £	Funding method	Disposal proceeds £	Disposal date
Motor vehicles							
Car CR04 YTR	01/04/X3	18,000.00			Cash		
Year end 31/03/X4			7,200.00	10,800.00	Cash		
Year end 31/03/X5			4,320.00	6,480.00			
Year end 31/03/X6			**2,592.00**	**3,888.00**			
Office equipment							
Desk OFF253	01/01/X4	10,000.00			Finance lease		
Year end 31/03/X4			375.00	9,625.00			
Year end 31/03/X5			1,500.00	8,125.00			
Year end 31/03/X6			**1,500.00**	**6,625.00**			
Workstation OFF783	01/12/X5	6,795.00			**Hire purchase**		
Year end 31/03/X6			**340.00**	**6,455.00**			
Workstation GT551	01/07/X3	5,210.00			Cash		
Year end 31/03/X4			586.00	4,624.00			
Year end 31/03/X4			782.00	3,842.00			
Year end 31/03/X4			**586.00**	**0.00**		**1,955.00**	**01/12/X3**

Working:

Depreciation on car CR04 YTR = £6,480.00 × 40% = £2,592.00.

Depreciation on desk OFF253 = £10,000.00 × 1/5 × 75% (to remove residual value) = £1.500.00.

Cost of workstation OFF783: Purchase price £6,500.00 + directly attributable costs £295 = £6,795.00 (as the company is VAT registered, VAT is not included in the cost of the asset as it can be recovered from HMRC).

Note. The printer paper is revenue expenditure so is not capitalised.

Depreciation of workstation OFF783 = £6,795.00 × 1/5 × 75% × 4/12 = £340.00 (as depreciation is charged on a monthly pro-rata basis).

Depreciation of workstation GT551 to date of disposal = £5,210 × 1/5 × 75% × 9/12 = £586.00 (as depreciation is charged on a monthly pro-rata basis).

Carrying amount of workstation GT551: this is cleared to 0.00 as the workstation has been sold.

(b)

	✓
Expected market value at the estimated date of its disposal	✓
Difference between its carrying amount and the estimated scrap proceeds	
Original cost less its depreciation to date	
Carrying amount plus its accumulated depreciation at any given time	

Task 2

(a)

(i)

£	976.00

Working:

	£
1 January 20X3: Cost	2,000
Depreciation (20% × 2,000)	(400)
31 December 20X3	1,600
Depreciation (20% × 1,600)	(320)
31 December 20X4	1,280
Depreciation (20% × 1,280)	(256)
31 December 20X5	1,024

Accumulated depreciation at disposal = £400 + £320 + £256 = £976

(ii)   Disposals

	£		£
Machinery at cost	2,000	**Machinery accumulated depreciation**	976
		Machines at cost	350
		Profit or loss account	674
	2,000		**2,000**

(b)

(i)

£	1,300.00

Working

Cost of new machinery = Part exchange value £350 + cash paid £950 = £1,300

(ii) The machinery at cost account will have a final balance carried down

of | £ | 17,350 | when the ledger accounts are closed

for the year.

Working

Machines at cost

	£		£
Balance b/d	18,050	Disposals	2,000
Disposals	350		
Bank	950	Balance c/d	17,350
	19,350		19,350

(c)

Account	Amount £	Debit ✓	Credit ✓
Depreciation charges	97	✓	
Fixtures and fittings accumulated depreciation	97		✓
Narrative:			
Depreciation charged for the year ended 31 December 20X6 for fixtures and fittings purchased 1 November 20X6			

··

Task 3

(a) Commission income

	£		£
Accrued income (reversal)	175	**Bank**	496
Profit or loss account	384	**Accrued income**	63
	559		559

(b)

(i)

	Increase ✓	Decrease ✓	No change ✓
Assets		✓	
Liabilities			✓
Equity		✓	

Explanation:

The accounting entry to reverse the accrued income is:

DEBIT (↓) Commission income (SPL) £175
CREDIT (↓) Accrued income (SOFP) £175

The debit to commission income decreases the profit for the year and therefore also decreases retained earnings and equity.

Accrued income is an asset account (amounts owed to the business) and therefore a debit balance in the trial balance.

Therefore, a credit to accrued income results in a decrease in assets.

The above double entry has no impact on liabilities.

(ii)

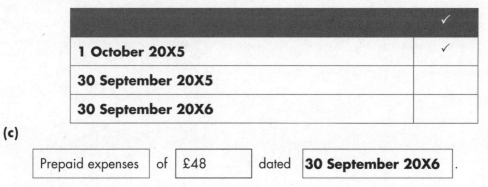

	✓
1 October 20X5	✓
30 September 20X5	
30 September 20X6	

(c)

| Prepaid expenses | of | £48 | dated | **30 September 20X6** | .

(d) £ 884

Working

Stationery

	£		£
Prepaid expenses (reversal)	134	**Prepaid expenses**	48
Bank	798	**Profit or loss account**	884
	932		932

Task 4

(a)

Account	Debit £	Credit £
Irrecoverable debts	672	
Sales ledger control account		672

(b)

Account	Debit £	Credit £
Drawings	850	
Suspense		850

Workings:

Should have done		Did do		Correction	
DR Drawings	£850	DR Suspense	£850	DR Drawings	£850
CR Bank	£850	CR Bank	£850	CR Suspense	£850

(c)

Account	Debit £	Credit £
Closing inventory – statement of financial position	9,205	
Closing inventory – statement of profit or loss		9,205

Workings:

Inventory should be valued at the lower of cost (£345) and NRV (£200) so a write down of £145 is required (£345 – £200).

This reduces total closing inventory to £9,205 (£9,350 – £145).

(d)

Account	Debit £	Credit £
Suspense	2,676	
Purchase returns		2,676

Workings:

Should have done	Did do	Correction
DR PLCA £1,338	DR PLCA £1,338	DR Suspense £2,676
CR Purchases returns £1,338	DR Purchases returns £1,338	CR Purchase returns £2,676
	CR Suspense £2,676	

(e) Complete the following sentence:

| I cannot | conclude that the balances included are now free from all

errors.

| I can | conclude that the inventory valuation as at 31 December 20X6

is included in the trial balance.

(f)

	✓
A client's sales manager wants you to accrue for a bonus based on the current year sales. The bank statement shows that the bonus was paid in the next financial year.	✓
A client wants to improve his profit figure. She asks you to delay recording a liability until after the year end.	
One of the client's credit customers is going out of business. You feel this news can be disregarded as the effective date of the business closure is after the year end date.	
Your firm needs to meet its deadline for preparing the final accounts. Your supervisor tells you to save time by using net realisable value for all items in the inventory valuation.	

Task 5

(a)

Adjustment	Amount £	Debit ✓	Credit ✓
Adjustment 1	1,489	✓	
Adjustment 2	1,267	✓	
Adjustment 4	180		✓

Explanation:

Discounts received reduce the amounts owed to our suppliers so are a debit balance. Cash payments again reduce what we owe our suppliers so are also a debit. Purchases returns are debited to the purchase ledger control account (PLCA) but here as the total was overcast, the PLCA has been debited by too much so a credit is required.

Adjustments 3, 5 and 6 require adjustments to the individual purchase ledger accounts rather than the PLCA.

(b)

	✓
Credit the allowance for doubtful debts account	
Debit the irrecoverable debts account	
Credit the allowance for doubtful debts adjustment account	✓
Credit the sales ledger control account	
None of the above	

(c) Extended trial balance

Ledger account	Ledger balances		Adjustments		Statement of profit or loss		Statement of financial position	
	Dr £	Cr £	Dr £	Cr £	Dr £	Cr £	Dr £	Cr £
Bank	5,246						5,246	
Capital		19,600						19,600
Closing inventory			6,712	6,712			6,712	6,712
Depreciation charges	4,298		4,000		8,298			
Discounts received		2,291		1,325		3,616		
Drawings	11,712		9,826				21,538	
Irrecoverable debts	627				627			
Motor expenses	2,065				2,065			
Motor vehicles accumulated depreciation		12,500		4,000				16,500
Motor vehicles at cost	20,000						20,000	
Office expenses	7,219				7,219			
Opening inventory	4,820				4,820			
Purchases	91,289				91,289			
Purchases ledger control account		7,109	786					6,323
Salaries	32,781		3,484		36,265			
Sales		156,782				156,782		
Sales ledger control account	11,092						11,092	
Suspense	12,771		1,325	14,096				
VAT		5,638						5,638
Profit/loss for the year					16,527			16,527
	203,920	203,920	26,133	26,133	**167,110**	**167,110**	**64,588**	**64,588**

BPP PRACTICE ASSESSMENT 3
ADVANCED BOOKKEEPING

Time allowed: 2 hours

BPP PRACTICE ASSESSMENT 3
ADVANCED BOOKKEEPING

Time allowed: 2 hours

BPP
LEARNING MEDIA

Advanced Bookkeeping (AVBK)
BPP practice assessment 3

Task 1

This task is about recording information for non-current assets for a business known as Tilling Brothers. The business is registered for VAT and its year end is 31 December.

The following is a purchase invoice received by Tilling Brothers:

Prestatyn Machinery Ltd 82 Main Road Perwith PE5 9LA	Invoice 654723	Date:	1 May 20X3
To:	Tilling Brothers 56 Kerrick Street Perwith PE4 7PA		
Description	**Item number**	**Quantity**	**£**
Press machine	MAC637	1	8,640.00
Delivery and set-up charges		1	300.00
Maintenance pack (1 year)		1	184.00
Net			9,124.00
VAT @ 20%			1,824.80
Total			10,948.80

This invoice was paid in full out of the business's bank account.

The following information relates to the sale of a desktop computer:

Identification number	COM265
Date of sale	1 January 20X3
Selling price excluding VAT	£850.00

- Tilling Brothers' policy is to recognise items of capital expenditure over £200 as non-current assets.

- Machinery is depreciated at 25% using the straight line method with a full year's charge in the year of purchase and none in the year of sale.

- Computer equipment is depreciated at 30% per annum using the diminishing balance method.

For the year ended 31 December 20X3, record the following in the extract from the non-current assets register below:

- **Any acquisitions of non-current assets**
- **Any disposals of non-current assets**
- **Depreciation for the year**

Show your numerical answers to TWO decimal places.

Use the DD/MM/YY format for any dates.

Note. **Not every cell will required an entry, and not all cells will accept entries.**

Extract from the non-current assets register

Description	Acquisition date	Cost £	Depreciation charges £	Carrying amount £	Funding method	Disposal proceeds £	Disposal date
Computer equipment							
Desktop COM265	01/01/X1	5,600.00			Loan		
Year end 31/12/X1			1,680.00	3,920.00			
Year end 31/12/X2			1,176.00	2,744.00			
Year end 31/12/X3			▼(1)	▼(2)			▼(3)
Laptop COM399	01/01/X2	7,200.00			Finance lease		
Year end 31/12/X2			2,160.00	5,040.00			
Year end 31/12/X3							

Description	Acquisition date	Cost £	Depreciation charges £	Carrying amount £	Funding method	Disposal proceeds £	Disposal date
Machinery							
Machine MAC434	01/07/X1	12,940.00			Part exchange		
Year end 31/12/X1			3,235.00	9,705.00			
Year end 31/12/X2			3,235.00	6,470.00			
Year end 31/12/X3							
▼(4)	▼(5)				▼(6)		
Year end 31/12/X3							

(1) Picklist for depreciation charges:

0.00
823.20
1,400.00
1,680.00

(2) Picklist for carrying amount:

0.00
1,064.00
1,344.00
1,920.80

(3) Picklist for date:

31/12/X2
01/01/X3
01/05/X3
31/12/X3

(4) Picklist for description:

Desktop COM265
Laptop COM399
Machine MAC434
Machine MAC637

(5) Picklist for date:

31/12/X2
01/01/X3
01/05/X3
31/12/X3

(6) Picklist for funding method:

Cash
Finance lease
Hire purchase
Loan

Task 2

This task is about recording non-current asset information in the general ledger and other non-current asset matters.

- You are working on the accounts of a business which is not registered for VAT. The business's year end is 31 December 20X3.

- On 1 January 20X3 the business part exchanged an old machine for a new one with a list price of £3,500. A cheque for £1,000 was paid in full and final settlement and this amount has already been entered in the cash book.

- The old machine cost £4,000 on 1 January 20X1.

- The business's depreciation policy for machinery is 20% using the diminishing balance method.

(a) Make entries to account for the disposal of the old machine and acquisition of the new one.

On each account, show clearly the balance carried down or transferred to the statement of profit or loss.

Machines at cost

	£		£
Balance b/d	12,500	▼	
▼		▼	
▼		▼	

Machines accumulated depreciation

	£		£
▼		Balance b/d	4,500
▼			▼	

Disposals

	£		£
▼		▼	
▼		▼	
▼		▼	

Picklist:

Balance b/d
Balance c/d
Bank
Depreciation charges
Disposals
Machines accumulated depreciation
Machines at cost
Machines running expenses
Profit or loss account
Purchases
Purchases ledger control account
Sales
Sales ledger control account

(b) **When a non-current asset is acquired by paying a regular monthly amount over a set period and then having ownership transferred at the end of that period, the funding method is described as:**

	✓
Cash purchase	
Hire purchase	
Loan	
Part exchange	

Task 3

This task is about ledger accounting including accruals and prepayments and ethical principles.

(a) **Enter the figures given in the table below in the appropriate trial balance columns.**

Do not enter zeros in unused column cells.

Do not enter any figures as negatives.

Extract from trial balance as at 30 June 20X4

Account	Ledger balance £	Trial balance Debit £	Trial balance Credit £
Administration costs	6,940		
Capital	7,300		
Sales returns	456		
Sundry income	1,050		

You are working on the final accounts of a business for the year ended 31 December 20X3. In this task, you can ignore VAT.

Business policy: accounting for accruals and prepayments

An entry is made into the income or expense account and an opposite entry into the relevant asset or liability account. In the following period, this entry is removed.

You are looking at rental income and heat and light.

Balances as at 1 January 20X3	£
Accrual of rental income	1,000
Accrual of heat and light	345

The cash book for the year shows receipts of rental income of £3,750. In January 20X4, the business received £500 in respect of rent for the month of December 20X3.

(b) **Prepare the rental income account for the year ended 31 December 20X3 and close it off by showing the transfer to the statement of profit or loss.**

Rental income

Details	£	Details	£
Accrued income (reversal)	1,000	▼	
▼		▼	

The cash book for the year shows payments for heat and light of £4,670. In February 20X4, an invoice for £1,290 was received in respect of the quarter ended 31 January 20X4.

(c) **Prepare the heat and light account for the year ended 31 December 20X3 and close it off by showing the transfer to the statement of profit or loss.**

Heat and light

	£		£
▼		Accrued expenses (reversal)	345
▼		▼	

Picklist for (b) and (c):

Accrued expenses
Accrued income
Balance b/d
Balance c/d
Bank
Heat and light
Prepaid expenses
Prepaid income
Profit or loss account
Purchases
Purchases ledger control account
Rental income
Sales
Sales ledger control account
Statement of financial position

You are preparing the year end accounts for another client. The client's bank calls you up and asks you to email them the draft accounts as they are trying to decide whether to extend the client's overdraft.

(d) **If you respond to the bank's request without permission from your client, which of the fundamental principles from the AAT's *Code of Professional Ethics* are you at risk of breaching?**

	✓
Integrity	
Objectivity	
Professional competence and due care	
Confidentiality	

Task 4

This task is about recording adjustments.

You are a trainee accounting technician reporting to a managing partner in an accounting practice.

You are working on the final accounts of a business with a year end of 31 December 20X3. A trial balance has been drawn up and a suspense account opened with a debit balance of £1,772. You now need to make some corrections and adjustments for the year ended 31 December 20X3.

You may ignore VAT in this task.

(a) **Record the adjustments needed on the extract from the extended trial balance to deal with the items below.**

You will not need to enter adjustments on every line. Do NOT enter zeros into unused cells.

(i) An allowance for doubtful debts of £2,420 is required at the year end.

(ii) A total column of £1,560 in the purchases returns day book was credited to the purchases ledger control account. All the other entries were made correctly.

(iii) Closing inventory for the year end 31 December 20X3 has not yet been recorded. Its value at cost is £12,860. Included in this figure are some items costing £1,250 that will be sold for £1,140.

(iv) A contra for £674 was debited to both the sales ledger control account and the purchases ledger control account.

Extract from extended trial balance

	Ledger balances		Adjustments	
	Debit £	Credit £	Debit £	Credit £
Allowance for doubtful debts		2,563		
Allowance for doubtful debts – adjustments				
Bank overdraft		265		
Closing inventory – statement of financial position				
Closing inventory – statement of profit or loss				
Irrecoverable debts				
Purchases	567,239			
Purchases ledger control account		81,272		
Purchases returns		8,922		
Sales		926,573		
Sales ledger control account	109,282			
Sales returns	4,982			
Suspense	1,772			

The ledgers are ready to be closed off for the year ended 31 December 20X3.

(b) **Show the correct entries to close off the sales returns account and insert an appropriate narrative.**

Account	Debit ✓	Credit ✓
▼		
▼		

Narrative:

	▼

Picklist for account:

Allowance for doubtful debts
Allowance for doubtful debts – adjustments
Bank overdraft
Closing inventory – statement of financial position
Closing inventory – statement of profit or loss
Irrecoverable debts
Profit or loss account
Purchases ledger control account
Purchases returns
Sales
Sales ledger control account
Sales returns
Statement of financial position
Suspense

Picklist for narrative:

Closure of general ledger for the year ended 31 December 20X3

Closure of sales returns account to the suspense account

Transfer of sales returns for the year ended 31 December 20X3 to the profit or loss account

Transfer of sales returns for the year ended 31 December 20X3 to the statement of financial position

You are now in the process of finalising the figures for the draft accounts. Your manager is concerned because there are no accrued expenses at 31 December 20X3 whereas at 31 December 20X2, accrued expenses amounted to £7,800. You are aware that the client is looking to retire and that a potential buyer has made a generous offer for the business.

(c) **Which of the following statements are appropriate in light of the above situation?**

Choose TWO.

	✓
The client may have deliberately omitted accrued expenses to maximise the offer from the potential buyer	
It is your duty as the client's accountant to maximise the sales price of his business	
Your manager should request a meeting with the client to discuss why there are no accrued expenses in the current year	
You should report the possible missing accrued expenses to the potential buyer of the business	

Task 5

This task is about period end routines and the extended trial balance.

You are preparing the bank reconciliation for a sole trader.

The balance showing on the bank statement is a debit of £800 and the balance in the cash book is a credit of £374.

The bank statement has been compared to the cash book and the following points noted.

1. Bank charges of £121 were not entered in the cash book.

2. A cheque received from a customer for £280 has been recorded in the cash book but it has been dishonoured and this has not yet been entered in the records.

3. A cheque for £765 to a supplier has not yet been presented for payment at the bank.

4. A direct debit of £650 to the local council appears only on the bank statement.

5. Cash sales receipts of £90 have been entered into the cash book but are not yet banked.

6. The bank has deducted a payment of £50 in error.

(a) Use the following table to show the **THREE** adjustments you need to make to the cash book.

Adjustment	Amount £	Debit ✓	Credit ✓
▼			
▼			
▼			

Picklist:

Adjustment 1
Adjustment 2
Adjustment 3
Adjustment 4
Adjustment 5
Adjustment 6

(b) Which of the following statements about the sales ledger control account (SLCA) is **TRUE**?

Choose ONE.

	✓
It is a record of amounts owed from individual customers	
Totals from the sales day book and cash book – debit side are posted to the sales ledger control account	
Sales returns will be recorded on the debit side of the SLCA	
Discounts received will be recorded on the credit side of the SLCA	

You are now working on the accounting records of a different business.

You have the following extended trial balance. The adjustments have already been correctly entered.

(c) Extend the figures into the statement of profit or loss and statement of financial position columns.

Do **NOT** enter zeros into unused column cells.

Complete the extended trial balance by entering figures and a label in the correct places.

Extended trial balance

Ledger account	Ledger balances		Adjustments		Statement of profit or loss		Statement of financial position	
	Dr £	Cr £	Dr £	Cr £	Dr £	Cr £	Dr £	Cr £
Accrued income			3,825					
Bank	7,281							
Capital		152,600						
Closing inventory			15,729	15,729				
Commission income		18,272		3,825				
Depreciation charges			27,600					
Drawings	40,000							
General expenses	67,298			1,427				
Motor vehicles accumulated depreciation		88,900		27,600				
Motor vehicles at cost	170,000		4,300					
Opening inventory	17,268							
Prepaid expenses			1,427					
Purchases	98,245			726				
Purchases ledger control account		14,681	710					
Salaries	69,256							
Sales		201,675						
Sales ledger control account	17,504			710				
Suspense	3,574		726	4,300				
VAT		14,298						
▼								
	490,426	490,426	54,317	54,317				

Picklist:

Balance b/d
Balance c/d
Gross profit/loss for the year
Profit/loss for the year
Suspense

BPP PRACTICE ASSESSMENT 3
ADVANCED BOOKKEEPING

ANSWERS

Advanced Bookkeeping (AVBK)
BPP practice assessment 3

Task 1
Non-current assets register

Description	Acquisition date	Cost £	Depreciation charges £	Carrying amount £	Funding method	Disposal proceeds £	Disposal date
Computer equipment							
Desktop COM265	01/01/X1	5,600.00			Loan		
Year end 31/12/X1			1,680.00	3,920.00			
Year end 31/12/X2			1,176.00	2,744.00			
Year end 31/12/X3			**0.00**	**0.00**		**850.00**	**01/01/X3**
Laptop COM399	01/01/X2	7,200.00			Finance lease		
Year end 31/12/X2			2,160.00	5,040.00			
Year end 31/12/X3			**1,512.00**	**3,528.00**			
Machinery							
Machine MAC434	01/07/X1	12,940.00			Part exchange		
Year end 31/12/X1			3,235.00	9,705.00			
Year end 31/12/X2			3,235.00	6,470.00			
Year end 31/12/X3			**3,235.00**	**3,235.00**			
Machine MAC637	**01/05/X3**	**8,940.00**			**Cash**		
Year end 31/12/X3			**2,235.00**	**6,705.00**			

Workings:

Desktop COM265

The accounting policy is no depreciation in the year of disposal hence the depreciation charge of 0.00. On disposal, the carrying amount is cleared to 0.00 and the disposal proceeds and date are recorded. The sales price is recorded net of VAT because the VAT must be passed on to HMRC.

Laptop COM399

Depreciation = 30% × £5,040.00 carrying amount = £1,512.00

Machine MAC434

Depreciation = 25% × £12,940.00 cost = £3,235.00

Machine MAC637

This is capitalised at its purchase price of £8,640.00 plus the directly attributable costs of £300.00 coming to a total of £8,940.00. The maintenance pack is revenue expenditure and as such should be expensed to profit or loss rather than capitalised. The asset is recorded net of VAT because as the business is VAT registered, it can reclaim the VAT from HMRC.

Depreciation = 25% × £8,940.00 = £2,235.00 as a full year is charged in the year of acquisition.

Task 2

(a) Machines at cost

	£		£
Balance b/d	12,500	**Disposals**	**4,000**
Bank	**1,000**	**Balance c/d**	**12,000**
Disposals	**2,500**		
	16,000		**16,000**

Machines accumulated depreciation

	£		£
Disposals	**1,440**	Balance b/d	4,500
Balance c/d	**3,060**		
	4,500		**4,500**

Disposals

	£		£
Machines at cost	4,000	**Machines at cost**	2,500
		Machines accumulated depreciation	1,440
		Profit or loss account	60
	4,000		4,000

Workings:

	£
1 January 20X1: Cost	4,000
Depreciation (20% × 4,000)	(800)
31 December 20X1	3,200
Depreciation (20% × 3,200)	(640)
31 December 20X2	2,560

Accumulated depreciation at disposal = £800 + £640 = £1,440

Part exchange allowance = List price £3,500 – Cash paid £1,000 = £2,500

(b)

	✓
Cash purchase	
Hire purchase	✓
Loan	
Part exchange	

Task 3

(a) Extract from trial balance as at 30 June 20X4

Account	Ledger balance £	Trial balance Debit £	Trial balance Credit £
Administration costs	6,940	**6,940**	
Capital	7,300		**7,300**
Sales returns	456	**456**	
Sundry income	1,050		**1,050**

(b) Rental income

	£		£
Accrued income (reversal)	1,000	**Bank**	**3,750**
Profit or loss account	**3,250**	**Accrued income**	500
	4,250		**4,250**

(c) Heat and light

	£		£
Bank	**4,670**	Accrued expenses (reversal)	345
Accrued expenses (2/3 × £1,290)	860	**Profit or loss account**	**5,185**
	5,530		**5,530**

(d)

	✓
Integrity .	
Objectivity	
Professional competence and due care	
Confidentiality	✓

Task 4

(a) Extract from extended trial balance

	Ledger balances		Adjustments	
	Debit £	Credit £	Debit £	Credit £
Allowance for doubtful debts		2,563	143	
Allowance for doubtful debts – adjustments				143
Bank overdraft		265		
Closing inventory – statement of financial position			12,750	
Closing inventory – statement of profit or loss				12,750
Irrecoverable debts				
Purchases	567,239			
Purchases ledger control account		81,272	3,120	
Purchases returns		8,922		
Sales		926,573		
Sales ledger control account	109,282			1,348
Sales returns	4,982			
Suspense	1,772		1,348	3,120

Workings:

Allowance for doubtful debts

The balance per the TB is £2,563. Therefore, a reduction of £143 (£2,563 – £2,420) is required. The necessary double entry is:

DR Allowance for doubtful debts   £143
CR Allowance for doubtful debts – adjustments   £143

Purchases returns

Should have done		Did do		Correction	
DR PLCA	£1,560	DR Suspense	£3,120	DR PLCA	£3,120
CR Purchases returns	£1,560	CR PLCA	£1,560	CR Suspense	£3,120
		CR Purchases returns £1,560			

Closing inventory

Inventory should be valued the lower of cost (£1,250) and net realisable value (£1,140). Therefore, a write down of £110 (£1,250 – £1,140) is required. This brings closing inventory in total down to £12,750 (£12,860 – £110). The double entry to post this is:

DR Closing inventory – statement of financial position   £12,750
CR Closing inventory – statement of profit or loss   £12,750

Contra

Should have done		Did do		Correction	
DR PLCA	£674	DR PLCA	£674	DR Suspense £1,348	
CR SLCA	£674	DR SLCA	£674	CR SLCA	£1,348
		CR Suspense	£1,348		

(b)

Account	Debit ✓	Credit ✓
Profit or loss account	✓	
Sales returns		✓

Narrative:

Transfer of sales returns for year ended 31 December 20X3 to the profit or loss account

(c)

	✓
The client may have deliberately omitted accrued expenses to maximise the offer from the potential buyer	✓
It is your duty as the client's accountant to maximise the sales price of his business	
Your manager should request a meeting with the client to discuss why there are no accrued expenses in the current year	✓
You should report the possible missing accrued expenses to the potential buyer of the business	

Explanation:

As a trainee accounting technician, you should be acting in the business's best interests rather than the client's personal interests. If you were to disclose the possible missing accrued expenses to the potential buyer, you would be breaching the fundamental principle of confidentiality from the AAT's *Code of Professional Ethics*. It is possible here that the client has deliberately omitted the accrued expenses in order to overstate the profit and maximise the selling price of the business. Therefore, as this is a delicate situation, it would be appropriate for your manager to arrange a meeting to discuss the matter with the client.

Task 5

(a)

Adjustment	Amount £	Debit ✓	Credit ✓
Adjustment 1	121		✓
Adjustment 2	280		✓
Adjustment 4	650		✓

Explanation:

Bank charges missing from the cash book will increase the overdraft with a credit. A dishonoured cheque from a customer needs to be removed from the cash book with a credit. A direct debit is a payment so results in a credit to the cash book.

Adjustments 3, 5 and 6 only affect the balance per the bank statement. Adjustment 3 will result increase the overdraft in the bank as it's a missing payment. Adjustment 5 relates to missing receipts so will reduce the overdraft. Adjustment 6 requires the reversal of a payment made in error so again will reduce the overdraft.

(b)

	✓
It is a record of amounts owed from individual customers	
Totals from the sales day book and cash book – debit side are posted to the sales ledger control account	✓
Sales returns will be recorded on the debit side of the SLCA	
Discounts received will be recorded on the credit side of the SLCA	

Explanation:

The amounts for individual customers are recorded in the sales ledger memorandum accounts. Sales returns will be recorded on the credit side of the SLCA rather than the debit side. Discounts are received from suppliers not customers so should be recorded in the PLCA not the SLCA.

Individual invoices and receipts in the day books are posted to the sales ledger memorandum accounts. Totals from the day books are posted to the sales ledger control account.

(c) Extended trial balance

Ledger account	Ledger balances		Adjustments		Statement of profit or loss		Statement of financial position	
	Dr £	Cr £	Dr £	Cr £	Dr £	Cr £	Dr £	Cr £
Accrued income			3,825				3,825	
Bank	7,281						7,281	
Capital		152,600						152,600
Closing inventory			15,729	15,729		15,729	15,729	
Commission income		18,272		3,825		22,097		
Depreciation charges			27,600		27,600			
Drawings	40,000						40,000	
General expenses	67,298			1,427	65,871			
Motor vehicles accumulated depreciation		88,900		27,600				116,500
Motor vehicles at cost	170,000		4,300				174,300	
Opening inventory	17,268				17,268			
Prepaid expenses			1,427				1,427	
Purchases	98,245			726	97,519			
Purchases ledger control account		14,681	710					13,971
Salaries	69,256				69,256			
Sales		201,675				201,675		
Sales ledger control account	17,504			710			16,794	
Suspense	3,574		726	4,300				
VAT		14,298						14,298
Profit/loss for the year						38,013	38,013	
	490,426	490,426	54,317	54,317	**277,514**	**277,514**	**297,369**	**297,369**

BPP PRACTICE ASSESSMENT 4
ADVANCED BOOKKEEPING

Time allowed: 2 hours

BPP PRACTICE ASSESSMENT 4
ADVANCED BOOKKEEPING

Time allowed: 2 hours

PRACTICE ASSESSMENT 4

Advanced Bookkeeping (AVBK)
BPP practice assessment 4

Task 1

This task is about non-current assets.

You are working on the accounting records of a business known as Markham.

You may ignore VAT in this task.

The following is an extract from a purchase invoice received by Markham:

Office Solutions Ltd Unit 7 Tenton Industrial Estate TN14 5YJ	Invoice 9746	Date:	1 March 20X3
To:	Markham 14 The Green Tenton TN3 4ZX		
Description	**Item number**	**Quantity**	**£**
Corner office suite	OF477	1	1,950.00
Delivery and assembly charges	For OF477	1	150.00
Printer ink cartridges		20	160.00
Desk lamp	DL234		110.00
Net total			2,370.00

The acquisition has been made under a finance lease agreement.

The following information relates to the sale of an item of factory machinery:

Identification number	MN864
Date of sale	1 July 20X2
Selling price	£1,050.00

- Markham's policy is to recognise items of capital expenditure over £500 as non-current assets.

- Office equipment and furniture is depreciated at 20% per annum using the straight line method. There are no residual values.

- Factory machinery is depreciated at 25% per annum using the diminishing balance method.

- Depreciation is calculated on an annual basis and charged in equal instalments for each full month the asset is owned in the year.

(a) **For the year ended 30 June 20X3, record the following in the extract from the non-current assets register below:**

- **Any acquisitions of non-current assets**
- **Any disposals of non-current assets**
- **Depreciation for the year ended 30 June 20X3**

Extract from non-current assets register

Description	Acquisition date	Cost £	Depreciation charges £	Carrying amount £	Funding method	Disposal proceeds £	Disposal date
Factory machinery							
Machine MN864	01/07/X0	15,600.00			Cash		
Year end 30/06/X1			3,900.00	11,700.00			
Year end 30/06/X2			2,925.00	8,775.00			
Year end 30/06/X3			▼(1)	▼(2)			▼(3)
Machine MN982	01/07/X1	9,400.00			Loan		
Year end 30/06/X2			2,350.00	7,050.00			
Year end 30/06/X3							

Description	Acquisition date	Cost £	Depreciation charges £	Carrying amount £	Funding method	Disposal proceeds £	Disposal date
Office equipment							
Server OF025	01/04/X1	12,940.00			Part exchange		
Year end 30/06/X1			647.00	12,293.00			
Year end 30/06/X2			2,588.00	9,705.00			
Year end 30/06/X3							
▼(4)	▼(5)				▼(6)		
Year end 30/06/X3							

(1) Picklist for depreciation charge for machine MN864:

0.00
2,193.75
3,120.00
3,900.00

(2) Picklist for carrying amount for machine MN864:

0.00
4,875.00
5,655.00
6,581.25

(3) Picklist for date:

30/06/X2
01/07/X2
01/03/X3
30/06/X3

(4) Picklist for description:

Corner office suite OF477
Desk lamp DL234
Machine MN864
Machine MN982
Server OF025

(5) Picklist for date:

30/06/X2
01/07/X2
01/03/X3
30/06/X3

(6) Picklist for funding method:

Cash
Finance lease
Hire purchase
Part exchange

(b) **Complete the following sentences.**

The non-current assets register is [▼] .

Checking physical non-current assets to entries in the non-current asset

register will enable the business to [▼] .

Picklist 1:

part of the general ledger
a list of the business's intangible non-current assets
part of the business's internal control systems
recorded in the statement of financial position

Picklist 2:

ensure that depreciation has been calculated correctly

verify that the double entries in the general ledger are correct

identify non-current assets not in the register or in the register but that do not exist

ensure all revenue expenditure has been correctly recorded

··

Task 2

This task is about recording non-current asset information in the general ledger and other non-current asset matters.

- You are working on the accounts of a business that is registered for VAT. The business's year end is 31 December 20X5.

- On 1 September 20X5 the business bought a new motor vehicle costing £15,000 excluding VAT. This was paid from the bank.

- The vehicle's residual value is expected to be £3,000 excluding VAT.

- The business's depreciation policy for motor vehicles is 20% per annum on a straight line basis. A full year's depreciation is charged in the year of acquisition and none in the year of disposal.
- Depreciation has already been entered into the accounts for the business's existing motor vehicles.

(a) Calculate the depreciation charge for the year on the new motor vehicle.

£ [   ]

Make entries to account for:
- **The purchase of the new motor vehicle**
- **The depreciation on the new motor vehicle**

On each account, show clearly the balance carried down or transferred to the statement of profit or loss.

Motor vehicles at cost

	£		£
Balance b/d	35,000	▼	
▼		▼	

Motor vehicles accumulated depreciation

	£		£
▼		Balance b/d	9,400
▼		▼	

Depreciation charges

	£		£
Balance b/d	6,300	▼	
▼		▼	

Picklist:

Balance b/d
Balance c/d
Bank
Depreciation charges
Disposals
Motor vehicles accumulated depreciation
Motor vehicles at cost
Motor vehicle running expenses
Profit or loss account
Purchases
Purchases ledger control account
Sales
Sales ledger control account
Empty

(b) **When non-current assets are depreciated using the straight line method, an equal amount is charged for each year of the asset's life.**

	✓
True	
False	

A business sells a motor vehicle and receives a part exchange allowance of £5,000 on a replacement vehicle costing £20,000.

(c) **Ignoring VAT, show the journal entry required to record the part exchange allowance.**

Account		Amount £	Debit ✓	Credit ✓
	▼			
	▼			

Picklist:

Balance b/d
Balance c/d
Bank
Depreciation charges
Disposals
Motor vehicles accumulated depreciation
Motor vehicles at cost
Motor vehicle running expenses

Profit or loss account
Purchases
Purchases ledger control account
Sales
Sales ledger control account
Empty

Task 3

This task is about ledger accounting, including accruals and prepayments, and applying ethical principles.

(a) **Enter the figures given in the table below in the appropriate trial balance columns.**

Do not enter zeros in unused column cells.

Do not enter any figures as negatives.

Extract from trial balance as at 30 June 20X4

Account	Ledger balance	Trial balance	
		Debit	Credit
	£	£	£
Purchases returns	8,400		
Discounts allowed	1,556		
Discounts received	2,027		
Office costs	2,950		

You are working on the final accounts of a business for the year ended 31 December 20X3. In this task, you can ignore VAT.

Business policy: accounting for accruals and prepayments

An entry is made into the income or expense account and an opposite entry into the relevant asset or liability account. In the following period, this entry is removed.

You are looking at interest income for the year.

• As at 31 December 20X2, there was an accrual for interest income of £750.

• The cash book for the year shows receipts of interest income income of £4,850.

• On 31 January 20X4, the business receives £900 of interest income for the quarter ended 31 January 20X4.

(b) **Prepare the interest income account for the year ended 31 December 20X3 and close it off by showing the transfer to the statement of profit or loss.**

Interest income

	£		£
Accrued income (reversal)	750		▼
▼			▼

Picklist:

Accrued expenses
Accrued income
Balance b/d
Balance c/d
Bank
Prepaid expenses
Prepaid income
Profit or loss account
Purchases
Purchases ledger control account
Rental income
Sales
Sales ledger control account
Selling expenses
Statement of financial position

You are now looking at selling expenses for the year.

Selling expenses of £1,445 were accrued on 31 December 20X2.

(c) **Complete the following statements:**

The reversal of this accrual is dated ⬚ ▼ .

The reversal is on the ⬚ ▼ side of the selling expenses account.

Picklist:

31 December 20X2
31 December 20X3
1 January 20X2
1 January 20X3

credit
debit

- The cash book for the year shows payments for selling expenses of £5,770.

- In April 20X4, an invoice of £3,180 was paid for selling expenses for the six months ended 31 March 20X4.

(d)   Taking into account all the information you have, calculate the selling expenses for the year ended 31 December 20X3.

£	

This is your first year of preparing the accounts for this client. The owner of the business asks you not to record the accrued interest income in the accounts for the year ended 31 December 20X3 as she is trying to reduce her tax liability. She offers you a free week in her holiday cottage if you do as she asks. You are very tempted as you have not had a holiday for a long time.

(e)   Which threat to the fundamental principles of the AAT's *Code of Professional Ethics* is most significant here?

	✓
Self-interest	
Self-review	
Intimidation	
Familiarity	

Task 4

This task is about preparing accounting adjustments.

You are the accountant preparing the final accounts of a business with a year end of 31 December 20X5. A trial balance has been drawn up and a suspense account opened with a credit balance of £2,098. You now need to make some corrections and adjustments for the year ended 31 December 20X5.

(a)   Record the adjustments needed on the extract from the extended trial balance to deal with the items below.

You will not need to enter adjustments on every line. Do NOT enter zeros into unused cells.

(i)   An allowance for doubtful debts of £3,200 is required at the year end.

(ii)   A total column of £1,885 in the sales returns day book was debited to the sales ledger control account. All the other entries were made correctly.

(iii) Closing inventory for the year end 31 December 20X5 has not yet been recorded. Its value at cost is £13,185. Included in this figure are some items costing £1,575 that will be sold for £1,400.

(iv) A discount received for £836 was credited to both the purchases ledger control account and the discounts received account.

Extract from extended trial balance

	Ledger balances		Adjustments	
	Debit £	**Credit** £	**Debit** £	**Credit** £
Allowance for doubtful debts – adjustments				
Allowance for doubtful debts		2,888		
Bank overdraft		590		
Closing inventory – statement of financial position				
Closing inventory – statement of profit or loss				
Discounts received		2,300		
Irrecoverable debts	790			
Purchases	675,564			
Purchases returns		9,247		
Purchases ledger control account		92,597		
Sales		843,898		
Sales returns	5,307			
Sales ledger control account	98,607			
Suspense		2,098		

The ledgers are ready to be closed off for the year ended 31 December 20X5.

(b) **Show the correct entries to close off the irrecoverable debts account and insert an appropriate narrative.**

Account	Debit £	Credit £
▼		
▼		

Narrative:

	▼

Picklist for account:

Allowance for doubtful debts
Allowance for doubtful debts – adjustments
Bank overdraft
Closing inventory – statement of financial position
Closing inventory – statement of profit or loss
Discounts received
Irrecoverable debts
Profit or loss account
Purchases
Purchases ledger control account
Purchases returns
Sales
Sales ledger control account
Sales returns
Statement of financial position
Suspense

Picklist for narrative:

Carrying down the balance on the irrecoverable debts account

Closure of general ledger for the year ended 31 December 20X5

Transfer of irrecoverable debts for the year ended 31 December 20X5 to the profit or loss account

Transfer of irrecoverable debts for the year ended 31 December 20X5 to the statement of financial position

You are now in the process of preparing the final accounts from the trial balance. Normally you have three days to do this but as you are about to go on holiday, you need to complete work in one day.

(c) **What type of period end pressure are you most exposed to in this situation?**

Choose ONE.

	✓
Pressure from authority	
Pressure to report favourable results	
Time pressure	
Pressure from stakeholders	

Task 5

This task is about period end routines, using accounting records and the extended trial balance.

You are preparing a bank reconciliation for a sole trader.

The balance showing on the bank statement is a credit of £3,050 and the balance in the cash book is a debit of £3,554.

The bank statement has been compared with the cash book and the following differences identified:

1. A standing order of £269 has not been entered in the cash book.

2. A cheque received from a customer for £500 has been recorded in the cash book but the bank has informed us that the cheque was subsequently dishonoured.

3. A cheque for £940 to a supplier has not yet been presented for payment at the bank.

4. A direct debit of £485 to an utility company appears only on the bank statement.

5. Cash sales of £330 have been recorded in the cash book but not yet banked.

6. The bank has credited interest of £140 to our account in error.

(a) Use the following table to show the THREE adjustments you need to make to the cash book. Enter only ONE figure for each line. Do not enter zeros in unused cells.

Adjustment	Amount £	Debit ✓	Credit ✓
▼			
▼			
▼			

Picklist:

Adjustment 1
Adjustment 2
Adjustment 3
Adjustment 4
Adjustment 5
Adjustment 6

(b) A debit balance on the cash book means that the business has funds available.

	✓
True	
False	

This task is about completing an extended trial balance and showing your accounting knowledge.

You have the following extended trial balance. The adjustments have already been correctly entered.

(c) Extend the figures into the statement of profit or loss and statement of financial position columns.

Do NOT enter zeros into unused column cells.

Complete the extended trial balance by entering figures and a label in the correct places.

Extended trial balance

Ledger account	Ledger balances		Adjustments		Statement of profit or loss		Statement of financial position	
	Dr £	Cr £	Dr £	Cr £	Dr £	Cr £	Dr £	Cr £
Accrued income			249					
Bank	7,281							
Capital		150,000						
Closing inventory			9,433	9,433				
Commission income		7,893		249				
Depreciation charges			14,600					
Drawings	10,000							
General expenses	42,932			765				
Machinery at cost	200,000		3,400					
Machinery accumulated depreciation		125,000		14,600				
Opening inventory	13,254							
Prepaid expenses			765					
Purchases	128,994			2,458				
Purchases ledger control account		17,493	399					
Salaries	75,606							
Sales		195,433						
Sales ledger control account	25,775			399				
Suspense	942		2,458	3,400				
VAT		8,965						
▼								
	504,784	504,784	31,304	31,304				

Picklist:

Gross loss for the year
Gross profit for the year
Profit for the year
Loss for the year

BPP PRACTICE ASSESSMENT 4
ADVANCED BOOKKEEPING

ANSWERS

Advanced Bookkeeping (AVBK)
BPP practice assessment 4

Task 1

(a)

Non-current assets register

Description	Acquisition date	Cost £	Depreciation charges £	Carrying amount £	Funding method	Disposal proceeds £	Disposal date
Factory machinery							
Machine MN864	01/07/X0	15,600.00			Cash		
Year end 30/06/X1			3,900.00	11,700.00			
Year end 30/06/X2			2,925.00	8,775.00			
Year end 30/06/X3			**0.00**	**0.00**		**1,050.00**	**01/07/X2**
Machine MN982	01/07/X1	9,400.00			Loan		
Year end 30/06/X2			2,350.00	7,050.00			
Year end 30/06/X3			**1,762.50**	**5,287.50**			
Office equipment							
Server OF025	01/04/X1	12,940.00			Part exchange		
Year end 30/06/X1			647.00	12,293.00			
Year end 30/06/X2			2,588.00	9,705.00			
Year end 30/06/X3			**2,588.00**	**7,117.00**			
Corner office suite OF477	01/03/X3	2,100.00			Finance lease		
Year end 30/06/X3			**140.00**	**1,960.00**			

Workings:

Machine MN864

This machine was sold on the first day of the year so there is no depreciation charge. The carrying amount is reduced to 0.00 on disposal. Then the sales proceeds and disposal date must be recorded.

Machine MN982

Depreciation = 25% × £7,050.00 carrying amount = £1,762.50

Office equipment OF477

Depreciation = 20% × £12,940.00 cost = £2,588.00

Office equipment OF477

The amount capitalised is the purchase price (which is over the capitalisation threshold of £500) of the corner off suite of £1,950.00 plus directly attributable costs of £150.00, coming to a total of £2,100.00. The printer ink cartridges are revenue expenditure so should be expensed to profit or loss. The desk lamp is not capitalised as it is below the capitalisation threshold of £500.

Depreciation = 20% × £2,100.00 × 4/12 (as asset was owned for 4 months of year) = £140.00.

(b) The non-current assets register is | part of the business's internal control systems | .

Checking physical non-current assets to entries in the non-current asset register will enable the business to

identify non-current assets not in the register or in the register that the do not exist

Explanation:

The other answers are incorrect because:

The non-current assets register is a list of tangible non-current assets (not intangible) and forms part of the internal controls system rather than the general ledger. As it is not part of the general ledger, it is not posted directly into the statement of financial position.

A physical verification of assets in the register will not verify whether depreciation has been calculated nor the correctness of the double entries (as it is not part of the general ledger) nor will it help with revenue expenditure as this is not capitalised as a non-current asset.

Task 2

(a)

£	2,400

Working:

(£15,000 – £3,000) × 20% = £2,400

Motor vehicles at cost

	£		£
Balance b/d	35,000	Balance c/d	50,000
Bank	15,000		
	50,000		50,000

Motor vehicles accumulated depreciation

	£		£
Balance c/d	11,800	Balance b/d	9,400
		Depreciation charges	2,400
	11,800		11,800

Depreciation charges

	£		£
Balance b/d	6,300	Profit or loss account	8,700
Motor vehicles accumulated depreciation	2,400		
	8,700		8,700

(b)

	✓
True	✓
False	

(c)

Account	Amount £	Debit ✓	Credit ✓
Motor vehicles at cost	5,000	✓	
Disposals	5,000		✓

Task 3

(a) **Extract from the trial balance as at 30 June 20X4**

Account	Ledger balance £	Trial balance	
		Debit £	Credit £
Purchases returns	8,400		**8,400**
Discounts allowed	1,556	**1,556**	
Discounts received	2,027		**2,027**
Office costs	2,950	**2,950**	

(b) **Interest income**

	£		£
Accrued income (reversal)	750	**Bank**	**4,850**
Profit or loss account	**4,700**	**Accrued income** (2/3 × £900)	**600**
	5,450		**5,450**

(c) The reversal of this accrual is dated ⟨ **1 January** ⟩ .

The reversal is on the ⟨ **credit** ⟩ side of the selling expenses account.

BPP
LEARNING MEDIA

(d)

£	5,915

Working:

Cash paid £5,770 – Accrual from prior year £1,445 + Accrual from current year £1,590 (3/6 × £3,180) = £5,915

Alternatively you could have prepared a ledger account:

Selling expenses

	£		£
Bank	5,770	Accrued expenses (reversal)	1,445
Accrued expenses (3/6 × £3,180)	1,590	Profit or loss account	5,915
	7,360		7,360

(e)

	✓
Self-interest	✓
Self-review	
Intimidation	
Familiarity	

Explanation:

Self-interest is the biggest threat here as you will personally benefit if you do as the client wishes. Self-review is not relevant as you are not reviewing any of your own work here. Intimidation is not relevant either as the client has not threatened you. Familiarity is unlikely to be an issue here as this is your first year working for this client.

Task 4

(a) Extract from extended trial balance

	Ledger balances		Adjustments	
	Debit £	Credit £	Debit £	Credit £
Allowance for doubtful debts – adjustment			312	
Allowance for doubtful debts		2,888		312
Bank overdraft		590		
Closing inventory – SOFP			13,010	
Closing inventory – SPL				13,010
Discounts received		2,300		
Irrecoverable debts	790			
Purchases	675,564			
Purchases returns		9,247		
Purchases ledger control account		92,597	1,672	
Sales		843,898		
Sales returns	5,307			
Sales ledger control account	98,607			3,770
Suspense		2,098	3,770	1,672

Workings:

Allowance for doubtful debts

An increase of £312 is required (£3,200 – £2,888 in the TB). The journal needed is:

DR Allowance for doubtful debts – adjustments   £312
CR Allowance for doubtful debts   £312

Sales returns

Should have done	Did do	Correction
DR Sales returns £1,885	DR Sales returns £1,885	DR Suspense £3,770
CR SLCA £1,885	DR SLCA £1,885	CR SLCA £3,770
	CR Suspense £3,770	

Closing inventory

Inventory should be valued at the lower of cost (£1,575) and NRV (£1,400). As NRV is lower, a write down of £175 (£1,575 – £1,400) is required. This brings closing inventory to £13,185 – £175 = £13,010.

The double entry required is:

DR Closing inventory – statement of financial position   £13,010
CR Closing inventory – statement of profit or loss   £13,010

Discount received

Should have done	Did do	Correction
DR PLCA £836	DR Suspense £1,672	DR PLCA £1,672
CR Discounts received £836	CR PLCA £836	CR Suspense £1,672
	CR Discounts received £836	

(b)

Account	Debit £	Credit £
Profit or loss account	**790**	
Irrecoverable debts		**790**

Narrative:

Transfer of irrecoverable debts for year ended 31 December 20X5 to the profit or loss account

(c)

	✓
Pressure from authority	
Pressure to report favourable results	
Time pressure	✓
Pressure from stakeholders	

Task 5

(a)

Adjustment	Amount £	Debit ✓	Credit ✓
Adjustment 1	269		✓
Adjustment 2	500		✓
Adjustment 4	485		✓

Explanation:

Adjustments 3, 5 and 6 are all to the balance per the bank statement – adjustment 3 will decrease the balance by £940, adjustment 5 will increase the balance by £330 and adjustment 6 will reduce the balance by £140.

(b)

	✓
True	✓
False	

(c) Extended trial balance

Ledger account	Ledger balances		Adjustments		Statement of profit or loss		Statement of financial position	
	Dr £	Cr £	Dr £	Cr £	Dr £	Cr £	Dr £	Cr £
Accrued income			249				249	
Bank	7,281						7,281	
Capital		150,000						150,000
Closing inventory			9,433	9,433		9,433	9,433	
Commission income		7,893		249		8,142		
Depreciation charges			14,600		14,600			
Drawings	10,000						10,000	
General expenses	42,932			765	42,167			
Machinery at cost	200,000		3,400				203,400	
Machinery accumulated depreciation		125,000		14,600				139,600
Opening inventory	13,254				13,254			
Prepaid expenses			765				765	
Purchases	128,994			2,458	126,536			
Purchases ledger control account		17,493	399					17,094
Salaries	75,606				75,606			
Sales		195,433				195,433		
Sales ledger control account	25,775			399			25,376	
Suspense	942		2,458	3,400				
VAT		8,965						8,965
Loss for the year						59,155	59,155	
	504,784	504,784	31,304	31,304	**272,163**	**272,163**	**315,659**	**315,659**